# FROM JIHAD TO JESUS

## JERRY RASSAMNI

LIVING
INK
BOOKS
*Writing Worth Reading*

ISBN 0-89957-091-7

First printing—July 2006

Printed in the United States of America
12 11 10 09 08 07   −D− 8 7 6 5 4 3

To Jennifer—my wife, my love,
and my partner in the journey of life…
You complete me…

# Contents

Lord, make me an instrument of Thy Peace;
where there is hatred, let me sow love;
where there is injury, pardon;
where there is doubt, faith;
where there is despair, hope;
where there is darkness, light;
and where there is sadness, joy.
O Divine Master,
grant that I may not so much seek to be consoled as to console;
to be understood, as to understand;
to be loved, as to love;
for it is in giving that we receive,
it is in pardoning that we are pardoned,
and it is in dying that we are born to Eternal Life.
Amen.


PRAYER OF ST. FRANCIS OF ASSISI

# Acknowledgments

F irst, I would like to acknowledge the love of God, the grace of His Son, and the fellowship of His Holy Spirit who sustain me daily. How I long to be with you forever in heaven...

I want to extend a special and sincere thank you to my wife and children who put up with my writing for endless hours on evenings, weekends, and holidays. Without your support and encouragement, this book would not have been possible. I would be remiss if I did not thank my deceased mother who always believed in me and who taught me how to give. Thank you to my relatives who still love and accept me after I became a Christian.

I would like to acknowledge the Muslims of the world. I love you from the inner depths of my spirit. I wrote this book to you because I have some good news for you. You do not have to spend the rest of your lives fearing the Day of Judgment as I used to. Christ has already atoned for your sins. All you have to do is to confess and repent of your sins, invite Christ into your heart, and accept His free gift of eternal life. How I pray that you may know and experience the love, peace, and grace of the God of Abraham through His Son Yasuu' Al Massih (Jesus the Messiah).

Thank you to Ed McMichael for teaching the basic tenets of the faith and for playing a big part in my salvation. Thank you to Dr James Dobson from Focus on the Family for helping to lead me to the Lord. You are truly God's gift to this generation. Thank you Dr. Ed Young for being obedient to the leading of the Holy Spirit and leading me into the faith. I am blessed by your ministry.

Thank you Patricia L. Riggs for being an instrument of the Holy Spirit and for encouraging me to write this book after 9/11. Thanks to my agent Les Stobbe for faithfully guiding me along this journey and to my publisher Dan Penwell for his servant's heart and outstanding partnership in this project. Dan's efforts and those of his editing and proofreading team including Agnes Lawless, Sharon Neal, and Rick Steele made this project a reality. A special thanks is also due to Paul Conant for his editing/proofreading efforts and Jan Winebrenner for her invaluable guidance.

Many friends and servants of the Lord who stood by me and encouraged me deserve my deepest affection and gratitude. These include my pastor Randy Bailey, my Rabboni (teacher), friend, and role model. Thank you to Dr. David Shibley, President of Global Advance, a great man of God with a great vision for this generation whose love and compassion have truly blessed me. You are an inspiration to me. I would like to have a special mention of the elders and the associate pastor at my church, Pete (and Marcia) Kralyevich, who are making a great difference in the kingdom. I will always cherish your love and kindness. Thank you also for the love and support of my entire church family, especially my Sunday School class.

Thank you to all my closest friends for your encouragement, prayers, and support, and for always being there for me – Robert Starnes, Matt Shivers, Brent Cowan, Dennis Green, Lance Haynes, Eins Rodrigues, Steve Yount, Mark Edwards, Myron Barron, Tom Jackson, and Vince Shovlin. Thank you also to my friend Tod Hare for your assistance. I am a blessed man for having all of you as friends.

All of you bless me and lift me up with your love and support. I love you, and I pray God's richest blessings upon you.

# Introduction

*Therefore everyone who confesses Me before men, I will also confess him before My Father who is in heaven. But whoever denies Me before men, I will also deny him before My Father who is in heaven. . . . And he who does not take his cross and follow after Me is not worthy of Me. He who has found his life will lose it, and he who has lost his life for My sake will find it (Matt. 10:32, 33, 38, 39).*

## Battle-of-Nashville Attitude

A story is told of a man on a bus tour around landmarks of the antebellum South. The bus driver, who was covering the American Civil War Battle of Nashville, Tennessee, pointed out the sights: "Right over there," he said, "a small group of Confederate soldiers held off a whole Yankee brigade."

As they proceeded down the road, the driver said, "Over there, a young Confederate boy, all by himself, fought off a Yankee platoon."

This account went on for a while until finally, the man taking the tour said, "Didn't the Yankees win anything in the battle of Nashville?"

The bus driver replied, "Not while I'm driver of this bus, they didn't."

It is easy for us to get a Battle-of-Nashville attitude toward life. We change history to suit our prejudices; we promulgate historical inaccuracies to boost our pride. We romanticize the past and sometimes even the present.

"How was the party last night?" someone may ask.

"It was great," we reply.

The truth may have been that the party was boring, the food was horrible, and the host was rude. To top it off, we may have suffered from a migraine but didn't leave the party so as not to offend the host. Nevertheless, the fact that we do not always espouse the truth does not negate the truth.

Telling the truth may not be convenient, polite, or the politically correct thing to do, but that does not negate that truth exists, and that it lurks independent of our public relations campaigns, pride, and prejudices.

" 'What is truth?' said jesting Pilate, and would not stay for an answer," wrote Francis Bacon.[1]

Pilate stood toe-to-toe with truth, yet he had no desire to pursue it. Similarly, many, or even most people take inherited beliefs at face value and allow them to form who they are. They are not always interested in the truth. Like Pilate, some people have no time for the truth. The truth may be uncomfortable, painful, and embarrassing. Consequently, they proceed willfully blind and deaf on the path of life. They view life in terms of their narrow prejudices and idealism, especially where religion is concerned. However, if they had the courage to question other ideas against the backdrop of the tarmac of their respective roads, they would become either stronger in their beliefs or would see their folly.

In our quest for the truth, we must never be afraid to question— for not to question is slavery of the mind on the altar of ignorance.

It is the greatest irony that men and women live and die enslaved without ever peering beneath the surface, without looking for the truth. I could have lived and died as a slave to ideas I had cherished much of my life, if, like Pilate, I had not taken the time to look beneath the surface of those beliefs. Thankfully, I chose to examine the evidence in search of the truth.

## My Own "Battle of Nashville"

In my personal debate in the realm of religion, my own experiences forced me to be both objective and rational. Since I grew up in the turmoil of the civil war in Lebanon, I bore arms to defend my people and our corner of the universe against the infidels (Christians). I saw many of my friends and brothers in arms fall. In my youth, I stared death in the face; I sought the smell of gunpowder, for fighting became a sport to me, a high of sorts. However, in the process, I came to see something that many people never perceive in a lifetime. In my jihad, I came face-to-face with a frightening discovery: the true human heart. I saw it exposed behind the masks of piety, behind the lies of purity, and behind the sham of godliness, and I beheld the heart of darkness. I saw the evil that belies the human heart, and the horror of it made me dig for the truth.

Subsequently, I dared to question my own "Battle of Nashville" in my religious infrastructure. I had the courage to think freely, unencumbered by my tradition and idealism. I looked, and what I saw changed me forever. I now know that I was once deceived into looking within for answers and redemption, but I am now redeemed into looking at Him who formed me and who knew me before He laid the foundations of the world.

This book contains my excavation of the truth and emancipation from the shackles of pride and idealism. This journey is not for the faint of heart, nor the automaton, but it's for the bold seeker of truth who cannot be silenced and burns within himself, no matter the price.

## The Framework of This Book

This book opens with my personal testimony of how I came to know Christ as my Savior and presents the evidence that led me to abandon Islam. In the same way that Islam boasts of its five pillars of the faith, my five exposition pillars of Islam are:

**People**—Are people born in fitrah? Do they need a Savior?
**The Qur'an**—Is it the true word of God?
**Muhammad**—Was he a biblical prophet?
**Allah**—Is he the God of the Bible?
**Ahadith** (Muslim customs and beliefs)—Are they from God?

These five pillars personify how Islam self-destructs once exposed to the flames of objective reasoning and critical analysis. It is no surprise that Muslim theologians have snuffed out analytical inquiry of Islam in order to shield it from its deficiencies. It is those whose faith is based on blind emotion rather than deep conviction that resort to barbarity instead of civility and the free exchange of ideas. If Islam is rational, well grounded, and cogent, then the debate will clearly strengthen it.

Although this book exposes the skeletons of Islam, its message, however, is one of love, hope, and redemption. God loves all people with a burning intensity. He wants everyone to experience the salvation that He freely offers through the death and resurrection of His Son, so that all may come before Him and call Him "Abba, Father."

# ONE

# How I Came to Know Christ as My Savior

*"I deserved to be damned in hell, but God interfered."*

—JOHN ALLEN[1]

## A Tale of Hatred

Hatred brewed in me on that peaceful day at the military front. I heard the church bells signaling worship and was incensed. Why shouldn't I be? Didn't the Christians spark the civil war in Lebanon, bent on the destruction of my people? Didn't they slaughter my kindred? Weren't they after our land? My hatred was not passive; it shook the foundations of my existence and swept over me like a tidal wave. This hatred demanded action. It demanded blood sacrifices on its altar.

From my bunker, I could see a man tolling the bell a few hundred feet away from me. Without hesitation, I took my sniper rifle with a long scope and aimed it at him. I thought, *Allah must be smiling on me.* After a deep breath, with my heart pumping and my adrenaline rushing, I had his head in my crosshairs and fired.

I screeched in horror and disgust! I could snipe a standing AK47 bullet from two hundred feet with my collapsible assault rifle! However, this time my skilled marksmanship failed me. What luck this man had! I couldn't believe that the bullet missed the man's head and smoked the wall only inches above as he bent down with the pull of the bell, and then ran for his life. I was distraught; I had missed the opportunity of a lifetime.

*This could have been the perfect conversation piece on my CB radio on quiet nights*, I thought to myself. I would have bragged to the Christians on the other side that I was the one who blessed their church service on that peaceful Sunday. I could have warned them that this would be the fate of anyone who dared toll a church bell or enter a church. Now all was lost because of my reckless arrogance and miscalculation. I thought to myself, *If only I had aimed at his body instead of his head, I would have shot him.* Maybe Allah wasn't smiling on me after all.

## My "Battle-of-Nashville" Attitude

I was born in Liberia, West Africa, of Lebanese parents who were Druze Muslims. The Druze are a small monotheistic group that was founded out of the Ismaili branch of Shi'a Islam by Al Hakim, the sixth Fatimid caliph (AD 996–1021).[2] Even as a nominal Muslim, I grew up believing that my faith was the only way of salvation and that everyone not believing it was doomed to hell.

When I was a few years old, my parents decided that my mother should move us to Lebanon, our ancestral land, so my siblings and I could attend school there. I grew up in one of the most beautiful, yet the most explosive part of the world—the Middle East.

My father, however, stayed in Liberia to tend his business and visited us occasionally. I loved my father as much as one human being can love another. When he was around, I was his constant shadow. However, when I was eight years old, he died of cancer.

Since I was very young when my father died, my mother did-n't allow me to attend the funeral. As a result, I did not have clo-sure at the time of his death. At first, I refused to believe that he was forever gone. I would rush to the door whenever I heard the doorbell ring for the next couple of years hoping that he might be at the door. The pain was so great; it was as if my heart was ripped out of my chest. It was as if I had died a thousand deaths. It was like pure darkness had penetrated my soul and left me chilled. The smallest memory of him would trigger an avalanche of tears. I missed him so much. I wished I could bring him back from death to life. It was pure agony. It was the essence of pain. And for many nights and for many years, I cried myself to sleep. I was angry with God. I asked Him, "Why did You take my father from me?"

## My Physical Jihad

By the 1970s, tension was rising in Lebanon due to the failure of the dominant Christians to update the 1932 census—which was the basis for the allocation of power—in favor of faster-growing Muslims. To add to this tension, following its expulsion from Jordan in 1971, the Palestine Liberation Organization (PLO) established itself in Lebanon as a powerful military force. The influx of this large Palestinian community with heavily armed commandos upset the relatively fragile political balance in Lebanon. On April 13, 1975, in response to a drive-by killing of four of their members by sus-pected Palestinians, Phalange militiamen (radical rightist Christian Party dominated by Maronite/Catholics) pulled over a bus full of twenty-seven Palestinian workers, and slit their throats in what became known as the Bus Massacre or Ayn Rummaneh Massacre.

Furthermore, on Saturday, December 6, 1975, in retaliation for the murder of another four of their members, the Phalange began an orgy of bloodshed against Muslims. The armed Phalange militias instituted checkpoints on major roads and intercepted passing cars and pedestrians in search of non-Christians. Since Lebanese identification cards showed religious affiliation, captured individuals were forced to show their identification cards. Any Muslims or Palestinians found were executed on the spot. As refugees, Palestinians did not carry Lebanese ID cards, hence, hundreds of victims were slaughtered in the span of a few hours. That day became known as "Black Saturday." It was the watershed event that kicked off the Lebanese civil war.

Once the leftist Lebanese National Movement (LNM – Muslim and Palestinian) coalition led by the Druze leader, Kamal Jumblatt, attacked Phalangist positions in response to this event. As a result, the Lebanese civil war, which was to last for fifteen years until 1990, was in full swing. Kamal Jumblatt was eventually killed in 1977 at the hands of Syrian agents.

More than 100,000 people were killed in this war and another 100,000 handicapped. Up to one-fifth of the prewar population, or about one million people, were displaced from their homes. Hundreds of thousands emigrated permanently. Most of the hostages taken, numbering in the tens of thousands, disappeared never to be heard from again. Thousands of land mines remain buried in the previously contested areas. Car bombs became a favored weapon of violent groups worldwide, following their frequent use during the Lebanese civil war. It is estimated that in the fifteen years of strife, there were at least 3,641 car bombs that left 4,386 people dead and thousands more injured.[3]

> In 1975, the Lebanese civil war, which was to last for fifteen years (until 1990), was in full swing.

Our enemies in this war were the Phalange (Catholic militias) whom the Israelis funded, armed, and trained. After the Israeli invasion of Lebanon in 1982, the Maronite Christian militias, under the cover of and with the blessings of the Israelis, went into the Palestinian camps of the Sabra and Shateela and slaughtered every man, woman, and child. These same militias invaded the Lebanese mountains where my people lived in order to annihilate us and throw us into the sea.

The civil war in Lebanon was a war of survival for my people, and as it progressed, I became more angry, ruthless, and fearless. I bore arms in my Jihad to defend our people against the infidels. Physical Jihad in Islam is traditionally a holy war or the physical struggle on the battlefield against one's enemies in order to ward off aggression.

My code name was Astro. I thought it was cool. I didn't do drugs. Somehow, I knew that drugs were bad for me—that they killed. I had an addiction of a different kind, however. Frequently, it manifested itself in an AK47 assault rifle, and at other times with a B7 (RBG) antitank, above-shoulder missile or with a B10 mounted artillery. Sometimes it was a grenade and at other times a land mine. At other times, it was a sniper rifle with a long scope or a handgun. Whatever it was, it had gunpowder in it.

In order to know why I had such a vile addiction, you must walk in my shoes. I lost the father I loved at the age of eight. My schooling was constantly interrupted with a loud siren as Israeli airplanes invaded my country's airspace to spy and bomb at will. My childhood came to a halt as a vicious civil war broke out. Tens of thousands were slaughtered. Death was everywhere. Buildings developed loads of cavities. Daily bombings and bomb shelters became an unpleasant fact. Nerves were on the edge. Hearts were racing. My enemy wanted me dead.

When I turned fifteen, I became a man. At least I thought I did. My enemy was still at the gate, and he wanted me dead. I trained to defend our land and existence. I had to kill or be killed. Gunpowder became my outlet, my escape, my addiction. When I was first baptized by fire in the heat of battle, I was gripped by fear for I knew that my life could be snuffed out in an instant. Soon, I gained a taste, a hunger for gunpowder. It was no longer good enough for me to wait for the action, but I had to create and escalate it. I went to fronts when they were quiet to begin skirmishes. I would sit there in wait and snipe at my enemies to feed my addiction. I prided myself on my marksmanship, so when I was bored, I used phosphoric bullets and landed them inside enemy foxholes. I became like a heroine addict waiting for the next fix, the next injection to satisfy my adrenaline rush and animalistic urge.

Sometimes when I would begin a skirmish, I used B7 (RBG) to destroy my enemies' armed vehicles. When I got more firepower back than what I bargained for, I would call for reinforcements and heavy artillery came to my aid. At times, these unprovoked encounters turned into serious battles that I regretted, especially when my company was outgunned. However, somehow I survived.

When it was quiet on the military fronts at night, we gathered around radio CBs to speak to Christians on the other side. We blasphemed each other and everything the other held sacred. The names constantly on my lips during these vulgar exchanges were those of Jesus, Mary, and the priests. At that time, I thought I believed in God and that He sanctioned hatred.

One day, while at central command, we got word that two mounted enemy vehicles had just passed the militarized zone and were coming toward us. When we saw them, we quickly took the drivers out and then concentrated our firepower on the mounted machine gunners. Less than a minute later, all of them had fallen, but the bullets continued flying. The beasts in us took over. We didn't want this to end. Minutes later, two bodies were burning right in front of me. I heard the crackling of the flesh, smelled the burning tissue, and I was satisfied. The adrenaline was rushing. *Those pigs did not deserve to live,* I thought to myself. I remember the malevolence of the moment as we poked fun at their burning bodies and hurled insults at them.

**At that time, I thought I believed in God and that He sanctioned hatred.**

My humanity later returned from its sabbatical. I realized the fragility of life. God had created those human beings. They had dreams, and they had mothers, fathers, aunts, uncles, and perhaps siblings, wives, and children.

I came close to death on several occasions in the midst of fighting many battles. One day I was planting mines in a field when I saw a farmer boy approaching. In my haste to warn him of the impending danger, I accidentally stepped on a mine I had just planted. My heart sank! I knew that when I took my weight off that mine, it would blow me into oblivion! I spoke to God that day, and He must have heard me for I miraculously stepped away unharmed and so did the boy. Another narrow escape occurred when my company and I were trapped behind enemy lines. News had gotten to my mother that we were probably dead, but we escaped unharmed at dawn.

Weapons were like toys in my circle of friends. My brother, Sam, once pointed an AK47 assault rifle at my chest, thinking it wasn't loaded. Laughing and joking, he pulled the trigger, but inexplicably, the bullet did not fire!

I stared death in the face during another skirmish when I threw a hand grenade that caught in a tree in front of me. I could not run since bullets showered around me. I ducked and braced for the explosion, but it never came. Many of my friends were not so fortunate. In fact, I lost two of my closest friends in this war to Christian snipers' bullets, one in a skirmish at a front and the other while innocently playing soccer at an adjacent field.

As I grew up in the turmoil of the civil war in Lebanon, my mother found it increasingly difficult to control my brothers and me. We were the products of our surroundings. Filled with hatred, we became desensitized to violence and death. I saw dead men lying on the streets in pools of their own blood, no better than dogs. I saw the banality of evil that we each are capable of. I saw the dark hearts of humankind. I saw the darkness in my own soul and was changed by the horror of it.

> I saw the banality of evil that we each are capable of. I saw the dark hearts of humankind. I saw the darkness in my own soul and was changed by the horror of it.

War is not all it is cracked up to be. I saw my friends and brothers in arms fall—sometimes by the enemy and sometimes by friendly fire. I saw death around me and began to ask "why?" Why have we become instruments of darkness? Where did we lose our humanity? Why have we become worse than beasts in the jungle? At least beasts kill to eat, but a human kills to satisfy his hatred and thirst for blood. I began to understand that man is evil at his core, for he is capable of such untold evils that even wild beasts cannot top.

One day, I began thinking like a salmon. I started swimming upstream against the flowing current of hatred that violently pulls downward everything in its way. It's easy to float with the current but difficult to swim against the force of the river. I wanted out. I wanted out of this hatred, the killing, and the war. I wanted a future, a life. I knew there was more to life than this. I wanted to become educated. I wanted to marry and have children.

I always dreamed of going to America, of sharing in the American dream, but I couldn't leave the country since I was at military drafting age. I wasn't fond of the army since they were the puppets of the Christians, and because I fought against them on occasions. After my brother Sam was injured in the war, my mother was determined to get us out of the country. She was able to pro-cure a doctor's letter stating that I needed to leave the country immediately for Cyprus to have eye surgery. I wasn't in need of eye surgery, but it was an excuse to get me out of the country.

> **Evils are not foreign to man. They come from within.**

My heart was pounding as I presented my paperwork to the army at the airport on the day I was trying to leave the country. I thought, *What if they recognized my name? What if they knew that I shot at them not far from the airport?* The army immigration cleared me, and I was free to board the airplane. Instead of heading to Cyprus, I headed to Spain, and later to America in pursuit of a col-lege education. On the day I left my ancestral land, I opened a new page in my life. I came to understand that hatred is a vicious cycle that does not lead to results. Hatred is not an attribute of the Creator, but of the enemy of humanity. I saw the darkness in human beings. I knew the unrestrained evil that humans are capa-ble of and saw that there was nothing redeeming about humanity.

## A Tale of Love

While in Houston, Texas, away from exploding artillery and the specter of death, I met Jennifer. It was love at first sight. We were married six months later. Before she agreed to marry me, she made me promise to go to church with her. I thought that visiting church would be a win-win situation for both of us. I had always believed the Bible to be false, but did not know why. Studying the Bible would enable me to intelligently articulate why the Bible was in error. Therefore, I agreed to visit the church with Jennifer, but I forewarned her that I would never convert to Christianity.

> I saw the darkness in human beings. I knew the unrestrained evil that humans are capable of and saw that there was nothing redeeming about humanity.

Jennifer and I attended Second Baptist Church in Houston. Not long after we started going there, she learned that we were unequally yoked in marriage, referring to the biblical command that a Christian should not marry a non-Christian (see 2 Cor. 6:14).

After church one Sunday, she confessed to me, "Jerry, I really wish you were a Christian."

"I was born Druze, and I will die Druze," I replied with deep-seated anger. "And there is nothing you or anyone else can do to change me."

That was the end of that conversation. Jennifer and I never discussed it again.

After listening to a series developed by Focus on the Family called "Beloved Unbeliever," Jennifer knew she could not nag me into the kingdom of God or shove the gospel down my throat. Instead, she began to show me unconditional love while secretly praying that God would open my eyes and let me see my need of Him.

I thought, *Me, become a Christian? You must be kidding me! Christians ministered to me with bullets in Lebanon. Furthermore, Christ was a Jew.*

But Jesus had said, "If you have faith the size of a mustard seed, you will say to this mountain, 'Move from here to there,' and it will move" (Matt. 17:20). In other words, what is humanly impossible is possible with God. Prayer moves mountains.

## My Spiritual Jihad (Jihad Al-Nafs)

In Islam, there are several types of Jihad. The two major forms are a physical struggle against oppressors and a spiritual struggle for one's soul.

Jihad Al-Nafs is a personal non-violent, inward spiritual struggle to attain perfect faith. It is considered the Greater Jihad [jihad al-akbar].

The physical jihad is considered the Lesser Jihad [jihad al-asghar].

As a secular Muslim, I never thought in religious terms, but unbeknownst to me, I had begun a journey in a new kind of struggle—not of physical nature, but of eternal and spiritual dimension. It was a battle for the destiny of my soul.

> Unbeknowst to me, I had begun a journey in a new kind of struggle—not of physical nature, but of eternal and spiritual dimension. It was a battle for the destiny of my soul.

## God Is Love

Jennifer and I continued to attend Second Baptist Church. I even went to Sunday school with her. In fact, the class director, Ed McMichael, offered to teach me the Bible even though I had no desire to be a Christian. Wanting to intelligently articulate why the Bible was false, I agreed. Ed and I met twice weekly for ten weeks. His deep love for God and his coaching were instrumental in teaching me the basic tenets of Christianity.

It has been said, "You cannot separate truth from the one who preaches it to you."[4] Christianity would have crumbled in my sight if Christians did not live it. After spending time with Ed and other people from Sunday school, I saw something different about them— joy, peace, unconditional love, and compassion for others. I had previously thought that all Westerners were Christian, but these people lived their faith. They were far different from the so-called Christians who wanted to kill me in Lebanon.

> I learned that not everyone who claims to be a Christian is in fact a follower of Christ. True followers of Christ are marked by love.

The more I interacted with these followers of Christ, the more I wanted to understand what made them different. After examining the Scriptures, I understood their secret. It was encapsulated in the words of Jesus when He was asked to identify the most important commands: " 'Hear, O Israel! The Lord our God is one Lord; and you shall love the Lord your God with all your heart, and with all your soul, and with all your mind, and with all your strength.' The second is this, 'You shall love your neighbor as your-

self.' There is no other commandment greater than these" (Mark
12:29–31).

I learned that not everyone who
claims to be a Christian is in fact a
follower of Christ. True followers of
Christ are marked by love.

Jennifer continued to pray for
my salvation, and I examined the
Scriptures, coming across many revolutionary teachings. Islam uses
ninety-nine names of God, but not
one of them is "Love" or "Father."
However, I read about a God who

> Islam uses ninety-
> nine names of
> God, but not one
> of them is "Love"
> or "Father," but
> I realized that I
> could come before
> the throne of the
> Creator of the
> universe and call
> him *Baba* Father.

loved people so much that even after they rebelled against Him and
hated Him, He made a covenant with them to pay for their sins
with His Son's blood. If I accepted that gift of grace, I could come
before the throne of the Creator of the universe, and call Him *Baba*
(an affectionate word for Abbi in Arabic meaning father).

"The one who does not love does not know God, for God is
love" (1 John 4:8). Love cannot enforce itself by the sword, but it
rejoices in the truth (1 Cor. 13:6). Love is kind and gentle. It is not
easily angered, and it keeps no record of wrongs (1 Cor. 13:4, 5).

## Islam

The only time in its history that Islam was loving and tolerant was
when it was weak during the Meccan period. However, once Islam's
prophet immigrated to Medina, gained a larger following, and
became stronger militarily, tolerance was supplanted by fanaticism.
In one fell swoop, all the older verses that preached tolerance in the

Qur'an were replaced by the verse of the sword. Violence became entrenched as Islam's tacit mantra: *"And kill them wherever you find them, and drive them out from whence they drove you out . . ."* (Surah 2:191).

Moreover,

> In one fell swoop, all the older verses that preached tolerance in the Qur'an were replaced by the verse of the sword.

*Make ready against them all the power you can [gather], including steeds of war, to strike terror into [the hearts of] the enemies of Allah and your enemies* (Surah 8:60).

*So when the sacred months have passed away, then slay the idolaters wherever you find them, and take them captives and besiege them and lie in wait for them in every ambush* (Surah 9:5).

*The punishment of those who wage war against Allah and His apostle and strive to make mischief in the land is only this, that they should be murdered or crucified or their hands and their feet should be cut off on opposite sides . . .* (Surah 5:33).

It is not surprising therefore, that Islam's prophet engaged in a campaign of genocide against the Jews. Following Muhammad's death, it's only natural that Abu Bakr, the first caliph, used the above verses as the basis for using the sword to bring the tribes that had abandoned Islam back into the fold. In addition, the second caliph, Omar

> Islam grew not due to love but to the sword while spilling rivers of blood wherever it went.

Ibn Al Khattab, treated non-Muslims as second-class citizens, taxed them without limit, forced Christians to cut their hair, and forbade them to ring their church bells. As a result of the sword, Islam grew while spilling rivers of blood wherever it went.

> Islam commands its followers to live by the sword, when Jesus commands His true followers to turn the other cheek.

Islam commands its followers to live by the sword, when Jesus commands His true followers to turn the other cheek: "But I tell you, don't resist an evildoer. On the contrary, if anyone slaps you on your right cheek, turn the other to him also" (Matt. 5:39 HCSB). After asking myself which is the superior faith, I became convinced that loving one's enemies is superior to hating and killing them, praying for them is more righteous than cutting off their limbs, and turning the other cheek is more godly than murdering or crucifying them. I also was convicted that due to the darkness in the human heart, our tears, sorrows, and works could not undo the damage of iniquity and atone for our sins. For that we needed a savior.

As I learned more about the Bible, I began to think about my beliefs. The ugliness of war, coupled with human evil, contradicted Islam's message that people are born in a pure state and are

> After asking myself which is the superior faith, I became convinced that loving one's enemies is superior to hating and killing them, praying for them is more righteous than cutting off their limbs, and turning the other cheek is more godly than murdering or crucifying them.

basically good. Knowing the darkness in my own heart and having
seen it in others, I found myself
wondering: How could people,
who are capable of overwhelming
evil, have goodness at their core
and evil at the periphery as Islam
claims? Isn't it the other way
around?

If God forgave Adam for his
transgression as the Qur'an teaches,
then why weren't he and his descendants repatriated into paradise and
their fellowship restored with God? Why do we have to suffer the
consequences of sin, with lives marked by hardship, disease, and
death?

If we were really born in a pure state and subsequently corrupted by our environments as Islam claims, then why do we
never have to teach a child how to lie, be selfish, or cruel?

In this struggle of the mind, I realized that our fallen nature
cannot repair itself and undo the damage any more than a splat-
tered egg on the kitchen floor can unsplatter itself. We cannot
undo our fallen natures by pushing religious icons or following
religious pillars, unless we water
down God's holiness. I concluded
that we're in desperate need of
divine intervention and require a
Savior. Our sin is a clenched fist and
high treason against God's holiness,
and only the one against whom the
offense is committed can forgive

> If God forgave Adam for his transgression as the Qur'an teaches, then why weren't he and his descendants repatriated into paradise and their fellowship restored with God?

> I concluded that we're in desperate need of divine intervention and require a Savior.

our transgressions. (Incidentally, God's holiness is only mentioned twice in the whole Qur'an.)

## The Savior

Three things stand out in the life and ministry of Jesus Christ who is referred to as the Messiah in the Qur'an:

> *His birth.* He was born of a virgin even according to the Qur'an: *"She* [Maryam or Mary] *said: When shall I have a boy and no mortal has yet touched me, nor have I been unchaste? He (The Holy Spirit in physical image of a man) said: Even so; your Lord says: It is easy to Me: and that We may make him a sign to men and a mercy from Us, and it is a matter which has been decreed"* (Surah 19:20–21).

> *His life.* He was sinless even according to the Qur'an: *"He* (The Holy Spirit of God) *said* (to Mary): *I am only a messenger of your Lord: That I will give you a pure boy"* (Surah 19:19).

> *His death.* The grave could not contain Him, even according to the Qur'an: *"And peace on me* (Jesus) *on the day I was born, and on the day I die, and on the day I am raised to life"* (Surah 19:33).

The Jews wanted to crucify Jesus because He claimed to be the Son of God, the Savior of humankind. The Roman soldiers mocked Him, spat upon Him, and beat Him with heavy leather thongs armed with blades until His skin hung in long ribbons. His veins were laid bare, and His muscles and sinews were left open to exposure. The soldiers pounded a crown of twisted thorns into His skull and made Him carry His cross to Golgotha over his lacerated skin and mangled flesh, leaving a trail of blood behind. The soldiers pushed Him beyond the limitations of human endurance as they nailed Him to the cross. He had to push on the weight of the nails in his hands and feet to catch each breath, but despite all of this, He said, "Father, forgive them for they do not know what they are doing" (Luke 23:34). Finally, He said, "It is finished" (John 19:30)

> With every mocking, blow, step, drop of blood, pounding of the nails, breath, and every tear, God was saying to a fallen creation, "I love you. I love you. I love you."

and gave up His spirit. He was buried, rose from the dead on the third day, and appeared to many. In all of this, prophecy after prophecy that foretold of the Messiah was fulfilled. With every mocking, every blow, every step, every drop of blood, every pounding of the nails, breath, and every tear, God was saying to a fallen creation, "I love you. I love you. I love you."

It is no surprise that they crucified Him. The Bible predicted hundreds of years before the Persians invented crucifixion that the Messiah would be crucified. Crucifixion is believed to be the most painful death ever invented by humankind. It was such a painful death, that the English language derived the word *excruciating* from it. The Romans reserved this form of punishment for the vilest of criminals. Romans later stopped using it because it was so cruel. Jesus suffered such a merciless death because that is precisely the punishment that we deserve for sinning against the holiness of God. The eternal justice and integrity of God demand that the penalty for sin is death (Rom. 6:23). Thus, He (Jesus) who knew no sin, bore our sin so that we may be reconciled with God (2 Cor. 5:21). His suffering was according to the master plan that God revealed to Adam that the Messiah will suffer for the salvation of mankind (Gen. 3:15).

> Jesus suffered such a merciless death because that is precisely the punishment that we deserve for sinning against the holiness of God.

It was the greatest love story in the universe, where instead of wiping His creation off the face of the earth with His righteous wrath, the Creator pled with His rebellious creation, saying, "Stop. Stop. You don't have to go to hell. As promised, I already paid the price for your sin, hatred, and rebellion."

Jesus was God incarnate; for He was perfect as only God is perfect. He never sinned, and He never lifted a sword. He was the Prince of Peace who said to all who followed Him: "Love your enemies and pray for those who persecute you, so that you may be sons of your Father who is in heaven" (Matt. 5:44). Six centuries later, Islam adopted 70 percent of the Qur'an from the Bible, yet omitted God's love and grace. Islam proselytized people with the sword, the very symbol of human sin, hatred, and darkness.

> Islam adopted 70 percent of the Qur'an from the Bible, yet omitted God's love and grace. Islam proselytized people with the sword, the very symbol of human sin, hatred, and darkness.

What a contrast between religion and Christianity, law and grace, sword and love, empty words and miracles; but most of all, what a contrast between a skeleton lying in a tomb in Medina and an empty tomb in Jerusalem! It wasn't by accident that Jesus hung on a cross.

It wasn't by accident that He rose again. It was all part of a master plan to save a fallen humanity that could not save itself (Gen. 22:8). At the heart of that plan was grace: "He [God] made Him [Jesus] who knew no sin to be sin on our behalf, so that we might become the righteousness of God in Him" (2 Cor. 5:21). After Jesus stretched out His arms on a cross as if to hug the whole world, He said, "It is finished!" (John 19:30). He fulfilled the covenant God promised humanity from the beginning of time. The price for my sins was now fully paid. The divine intervention had occurred, and the long-awaited Savior had arrived.

> It wasn't by accident that He rose again, but it was all part of a master plan to save a fallen humanity that could not save itself.

The Christian thanks God for his salvation and the Muslim thanks himself, for he is at the core and center of it through his works—God has nothing to do with it. In Islam, Muslims dethrone God and enthrone themselves. Men and women become religious robots who religiously pray five times a day, but whose hearts are vile with unconfessed and unrepented sin.

> Islam provided man with a manual to live but it never dealt with the sin— the root cause that separated him from a Holy God in the garden.

## A God Who Hears (Ishmael)

It is interesting to note that when Hagar was running away from her mistress, Sarai, the angel of the Lord appeared to Hagar and told her that she was with child whom she should name Ishmael which means God hears (Gen. 16:7–11). And it was Ishmael who became the father of the Arabs.

Since the evidence of the identity of Jesus was overwhelming, I became intellectually convinced that Jesus was indeed the Son of God. My skepticism dissipated with every passing day. The Bible, which I had studied for two years in order to dispute its message, convicted me of my sin and convinced me that God is not a God of hate but of love, but I needed to have a sign that God hears.

So one Sunday in church, when Dr. Ed Young, the pastor, gave the invitation for people to accept Christ into their hearts, I wanted to hear from God, so I silently cried out to Him, *If Jesus is really Your Son, if You want me to reject my Muslim heritage and accept Him, then send me a physical sign.* A few minutes later as we were leaving this sixteen thousand–member church, I heard someone running behind me in the parking lot saying, "Welcome, welcome!" I felt a tap on my shoulder. As I turned around, Dr. Young took me by the arm and said again with much passion, "Welcome, welcome!" As I looked into his eyes, I understood that God heard me. He answered the simple prayer I had prayed moments earlier. I thought, *Surely, Jesus is God's Son, and the pastor was God's servant.*

My whole life up to that moment flashed before my eyes. I saw that God had me in the palm of His hand, protecting me for such a time as this. He protected me, even when I blasphemed His holy name, because He wanted me to know Him as my Father, who, unlike my earthly father, would never leave me nor ever forsake me. He felt my pain and heard my cries in those sleepless nights after my father died. It was as though He had waited all my life to be my Father. The same hands that made the stars, the sun, the moon, and the earth, that hung them without strings and ordered their circuits, who also made me, wanted me to be His son and to call Him "Baba."

> The same hands that made the stars, the sun, the moon, and the earth, that hung them without strings and ordered their circuits, who also made me, wanted me to be His son and to call Him "Baba."

On the following Sunday, without my saying a word to anyone about how God heard me, this ex-Muslim militiaman left his baggage of hatred behind. I walked down the aisle at church and said, "I want this Jesus who died for me in my life." And when I said yes to Jesus, I could say with Paul, "Even though I was formerly a blasphemer and a persecutor and a violent aggressor. Yet I was shown mercy because I acted ignorantly in unbelief; and the grace of our Lord was more than abundant, with the faith and love which are found in Christ Jesus" (1 Tim. 1:13, 14).

> When I said yes to Jesus, I could say with Paul, "Even though I was formerly a blasphemer and a persecutor and a violent aggressor. Yet I was shown mercy . . ."

When Martin Luther answered a knock on his door, a person asked, "Does Martin Luther live here?" "No," Luther replied, "he died. Christ lives here now."[5]

I know that Jesus changes lives and turns hatred into love, for on the day I gave my life to Christ, I also died, and Christ began living in my human shell. This Christ said, "Love your enemies and pray for those who persecute you so that you may be sons of your Father who is in heaven" (Matt. 5:44, 45). I can personally attest that God turns wolves into lambs, blasphemers into worshipers, and idolaters into believers by the power of His marvelous grace.

> I can personally attest that God turns wolves into lambs, blasphemers into worshipers, and idolaters into believers by the power of His marvelous grace.

I will no longer hate, but I will love my enemies and pray for those who persecute me. I will never tire of telling people of the greatest love story in the history of the world, no matter the cost, that they will abandon their own strength as a god, leave their hatred behind, and come to the throne of grace. The gospel must be lived. To live it is to love.

### Laughter and Tears

On the day I accepted Christ and was forgiven of my iniquity, my atheist brother, Sam, asked me, "Why have you rejected your heritage and identity?" I told him of Christ who loved him so much that He paid the price for his sins by His death on the cross and subsequent resurrection. I told him of Christ by whose stripes we are healed, by whose blood we are cleansed, and by whose grace we

> The gospel must be lived. To live it is to love.

are forgiven. On the day I was baptized (the week after I accepted the Lord), Sam accepted the free gift of eternal life that Christ offers. God forgave him his sins as God forgives all those who repent and accept His grace. God's salvation was not contingent on anything Sam or I did, for we could never earn it in billions of years. Since we could never earn it, salvation is a gift that God freely gives to those who accept it by faith.

Several years later, Sam went to be with the Lord. Someone said that the soul would have no rainbow if the eyes would have no tears. In my journey as a Christian, I've had to grapple with the reality that I will still go through "the valley of the shadow of death" (Ps. 23:4). In His holy Word, God reminds us that we live in a fallen world that has been ravaged by sin, sickness, and death. Yet God has other plans to take away our every tear. If becoming Christians would cause our troubles to go away, then everyone would become Christians out of convenience. But the Lord wants us to trust Him and His promises. Glorious things await the believer:

THINGS WHICH EYE HAS NOT SEEN, AND EAR HAS NOT HEARD, AND WHICH HAVE NOT ENTERED THE HEART OF MAN ALL THAT GOD HAS PREPARED FOR THOSE WHO LOVE HIM (1 Cor. 2:9).

For eleven years, I prayed that my mother would come to know the Lord, and she refused. In the fall of 1999 my mother came to visit us, and I asked her: "Mama, isn't it time that you confess your sins, and surrender your life to Christ that you may know beyond the shadow of doubt that you have everlasting life?" This time, after all these years of faithfully praying for her salvation, my Mama didn't mock me. She simply said, "Yes."

As I knelt beside her and led her through the sinner's prayer, I thought how great, how awesome, and how faithful my God is—the One who created the universe and ordered its steps. He hears my prayer and really does care for me. God became more real to me on the day when He gave me my mother's soul as a precious stone in His crown. Just like the name Ishmael implies, God heard and answered.

I understood on that day that God, who is eternal, does not operate on human calendars. God is never late, but is always on time. My mother, who was a mother and a father to me, discovered she had terminal cancer a few months later. As I saw her suffer greatly, I rested in the assurance that she had put her faith in Christ and that she will spend eternity with Him. When I could no longer bear the pain of watching her suffer, I tearfully asked my sweet Jesus to take her home that very night. He did. Despite her suffering, she had peace and joy on her deathbed. She looked at the ceiling and with the joy of a child reuniting with her father after a long and tiresome journey, I heard her say her last words in Arabic, "You came for me" (see 2 Cor. 5:8).

Though I asked my God to take Mama home, I was overcome with pain. All the pain of losing my father many years ago was resurrected in my heart. I cried in agony at losing my mother, but I felt an indescribable peace, as I heard the voice of my heavenly Father in my spirit saying, "My son, I understand your pain. I am no stranger to pain, for I gave my Son so you can spend eternity with her. I am your father and your mother, and I will always be with you."

The Day of Judgment is the greatest fear a Muslim has—the greatest mystery to them is which way will the scales tip, in the favor of virtue or vice! When I was a Muslim, I feared that my own unrighteousness might convict me. In a way, deep inside, I knew that my own righteousness would not measure up to God's standards of holiness. Now that I am a Christian, I no longer live in fear. I no longer trust in my own righteousness to save me, but by faith I trust in the righteousness of God which will never fail me (see Eph. 2:8, 9).

> God made a way for me to see my mother again in paradise where there will be no sickness, disease, or death.

When my mother accepted the Lord, she asked for my late brother Sam's Bible which Jennifer and I bought him on the day he accepted the Lord—October 8, 1988. When my mother was ill in bed, I would read God's Word to her from that very Bible. As I began to deal with my grief of losing her, I asked my God to speak to me. I opened that Bible for answers. It divinely opened to some passages that Sam highlighted, in chapter eight of the book of Romans. God spoke to me on that day concerning many things:

> I only said goodbye to my Mama for a season, for I know that my God will reunite me with my mother by His marvelous grace.

So there is now no condemnation awaiting those who belong to Christ Jesus. For the power of the life-giving Spirit—and this power is mine through Christ Jesus—has freed me from the vicious circle of sin and death. We aren't saved from sin's grasp by knowing the commandments of God, because we can't keep and won't keep them, but God put into effect a different plan to save us. He sent his own Son in a human body

like ours—except that ours are sinful—and destroyed sin's
control over us by giving himself as a sacrifice for our sins.
. . . Yet, even though Christ lives within you, your body will
die because of sin; but your spirit will live, for Christ has pardoned it (Rom. 8:1–3, 10 TLB).

The Bible does not tell us that we will not go through storms
of life, but that when we do, Christ is with us. The Bible also tells
us not to get too attached to this life, for we must be ever ready
to face death for His sake at any moment:

Who then can keep Christ's love from us? When we have
trouble or calamity, when we are hunted down or destroyed,
is it because He doesn't love us anymore? And if we are
hungry, or penniless, or in danger, or threatened with death,
has God deserted us? No, for the Scriptures tell us that for
his sake we must be ready to face death at every moment
of the day—we are like sheep awaiting slaughter (Rom.
8:35, 36 TLB).

I opened my story with hatred. It's only fitting that I seal it
with love since God is love, and since love is superior to hatred:

For I am convinced that nothing can ever separate us from his
love. Death can't, and life can't. The angels won't, and all the
powers of hell itself cannot keep God's love away. Our fears
for today, our worries about tomorrow, or where we are—high
above the sky, or in the deepest ocean—nothing will ever be
able to separate us from the love of God demonstrated by our
Lord Jesus Christ when he died for us (Rom. 8:38, 39 TLB).

I am going to be with my Father God in the Holy City, and partake of the Tree of Life. I am going to walk on streets of gold and rejoin my loved ones—my father, mother, brother, and sister who have gone before me. My God shall take away all tears and right all wrongs. However, this is not through my own works, but through the Messiah, the manifestation of God's amazing grace on the cross of Calvary two thousand years ago.

> The message is this: God is love. And because He loves us, He sent His only Son to pay the price for our sin and rebellion so that we can have intimate fellowship with Him for eternity.

## Your Own "Battle of Nashville"

Jesus said in Revelation 3:20, 21: "Behold, I stand at the door and knock; if anyone hears My voice and opens the door, I will come in to him and will dine with him, and he with Me." Jesus has already paid the price for our sins when He said: "It is finished." He knocks on every heart—your heart and mine—but He does not force Himself on us, since He is a gentleman.

Therefore, I pray that as you examine the evidence, both methodically and systematically in the ensuing chapters, that you, too, will repent of your sins and invite Him into your heart as I did.

"Now to the King eternal, immortal, invisible, the only God, be honor and glory forever and ever. Amen" (1 Tim. 1:17).

# Are People Born in Fitrah? Do They Need a Savior?

*When Adam sinned, sin entered the entire human race.*
*Adam's sin brought death, so death spread to everyone,*
*for everyone sinned (Rom. 5:12 NLT).*

The issue of whether people are born in a pure state or in sin is a defining difference between Christianity and Islam. This is indeed the smoking gun, the evidence by which Christianity or Islam rises or falls. Christians believe that people are born in a sinful state and that they require a Savior, whereas Muslims believe that people are born in a pure state [fitrah] and that they are able to attain moral purity by their own merits. Knowing our genetical heritage might shed some light on our spiritual pedigree and help resolve this dilemma.

> Christians believe that people are born in a sinful state and that they require a Savior, whereas Muslims believe that people are born in a pure state [fitrah] and that they are able to attain moral purity by their own merits.

In *Alice's Adventures in Wonderland*, the king said to Alice, "Begin at the beginning . . . and go on till you come to the end; then stop." In order to answer the question about a pure state, one must also start at the beginning—but with Adam— and reach the end with him before they stop. Therefore, the question is: Are people born in fitrah (a pure state—the Islamic view) or in sin (hampered by the results of Adam's sin, also called original sin—the Christian view)?

> "Although he was purged from the garden of bliss for it, to Muslims, however, Adam's sin affected him and him alone. Thus, the Qur'an claims that man is born in a pure state until he commits a guilty deed."

Surprisingly, the Qur'an retells the story of the Bible concerning the events in the Garden of Eden. The Qur'an tells us that Satan tempted Adam and Eve (Surah 2:36) and caused their shame to be exposed (Surah 7:27). They were subsequently expelled from the garden because of their sin (Surah 2:38). Thus, by deduction, the Qur'an admits that by disobeying God, Adam and Eve not only affected their own destinies by being expelled from the garden, but they also affected the destinies of their progeny, the human race. Despite these overwhelming evidences, Muslims do not entertain the doctrine of "original sin."

### Did Adam and Eve's Sin Affect Humanity?

It's clear that Adam and Eve's sin had lasting consequences for humanity, for as a result, they lost their innocence and the close fellowship they enjoyed with God in the garden (Surah 2:31–33).

Muslims acknowledge that God responded to sin by ordering both Adam and Eve to descend "Ahbituu" from the garden (Surah

2:36). Thus, the personal relationship between man and God was severed, and according to both the Qur'an and Ahadith, the command to depart from the garden (Surah 2:38) was intended to cover all humankind.

## A Critical Analysis of Fitrah

Although Muslims believe that people are born in a pure state [fitrah], that very notion is at odds with the Qur'an. The Qur'an recognizes that sin is an integral part of human nature and that all humans are captive to its power: *"And I call not myself sinless; surely* [man's] *self is wont to command evil, except those on whom my Lord has mercy"* (Surah 12:53). But if people are captive to sin, doesn't that mean that sin is an integral part of the human nature?

> If Adam did not lose his innocence in the garden, and if man was indeed born in fitrah (a pure state), then why aren't Adam's descendants still being born in the garden until they commit a guilty deed?

The commentary by the renowned Muslim theologian and author of classic works on Islam, Maulana Muhammad Ali, concerning the above surah (12:53), makes the point that the righteous never attribute any good to themselves, but they attribute all good to God who is the great source of goodness. The next part of Ali's analysis of the above verse (12:53), discusses the following three stages in spiritual development, according to the Qur'an:[1]

1. *Ammarah* (Surah 12:53), which Ali equates to the lowest stage in human spiritual development, is synonymous with

the animal self when people submit to their carnal desires like brute beasts.

2. *Lawwamah* (Surah 75:2), which Ali refers to as the self-accusing spirit, is the narrowest departure from the narrow path that is like a cramp in one's conscience.

3. *Mutma'inaah* (Surah 89:30a), which Ali terms as the stage of perfection, is the stage when the soul is at rest in perfect peace, having attained the goal of perfection.

> If people are captive to sin, doesn't that mean that sin is an integral part of the human nature?

Ali concludes his analysis as follows: "Those who have attained the second stage in spiritual advancement and those who have attained the goal of perfection are spoken of as those on whom my Lord has mercy."[2]

It's troubling, however, to attempt to reconcile the Muslim's blind belief in fitrah with the above view of the spiritual enlightenment ladder:

1. Isn't it a contradiction in terms to state we are born perfect [fitrah] while we are born imperfect [Ammarah]? In other words, if we are born in fitrah (a pure state), then how can we also be enslaved and predisposed to sin by submitting to our carnal desires like brute beasts?

2. How can we achieve perfection [mutma'inaah] and

> We have all sinned and have gone astray from the straight path (Surah 1:5).

become godlike when only God is perfect? Isn't it blasphemous to claim that we can become like God?

3. If we have all sinned as the Qur'an claims (Surah 16:61; 12:53), then how can we achieve perfection unless we water down the standards of perfection? But if we dilute perfection, don't we also dilute the holiness of God?

4. If children are born pure and are subsequently corrupted by their environments as Muslims claim, then wouldn't that imply that they are born into mutma'inaah (perfection) and then degrade into ammarah (animal self) instead of the other way around?

5. Since the Qur'an does not offer the assurance of salvation to anyone except those who die in the cause of jihad, then what good is the stage of perfection [mutma'inaah] if it cannot guarantee salvation?

6. Al Bukhari reported in the Hadith that the prophet Muhammad used to ask for forgiveness of his sins seventy times a day.[3] Why would he do that if as Muslims claim he was "the perfect example to humanity," having no sin [mutma'inaah]? Was Islam's prophet not in mutma'inaah (perfection stage)? But if even Islam's prophet, who is purported to be the model of purity for Muslims, was not in the stage of perfection [mutma'inaah], then what hope do other Muslims have in achieving the stage of perfection?

Humans can never bear the load of moral perfection. People tried to carry that load in the Old Testament and failed miserably; this is precisely why God promised them a Savior. Islam did not learn from the past, but plagiarized a Jewish legalistic system that is doomed to failure in the quest for salvation because it put too great a burden on humans.

Let's contrast the above with the biblical view of one's moral state. The Bible speaks of three stages in this spiritual journey:[4]

> One can never bear the load of moral perfection. People tried to carry that load in the Old Testament and failed miserably; this is precisely why God promised them a Savior.

1. *Generation* (creation) which begins with Adam and Eve when they had fellowship with God in the garden. They had not yet sinned against the Almighty and had not been separated from Him (Gen. 2:15, 16).

2. *Degeneration* when Adam and Eve sinned against the Almighty. As a result, they were separated from God and expelled from the garden (Gen. 3:23). They died spiritually and began to die physically. Hence, the aging process began (Gen. 2:19).

3. *Regeneration* or the new birth, when people receive new life and become spiritually alive again. Jesus told Nicodemus, "Unless one is born again, he cannot see the kingdom of God" (John 3:3). As one in faith accepts Christ's sacrifice on the cross as an atonement for degeneration, that person is reborn or born again.

## The Cycle of Life and Death

Both the Bible and the Qur'an agree that God created humans, and they enjoyed a special relationship with the Creator in the garden, but that relationship was severed. As a result, the quest of religion is how to restore that broken relationship. But religion cannot restore it; only God can. The Bible says that without faith it is impossible to please God (Heb. 11:6). The following paragraphs offer some insights concerning the creation, degeneration, and regeneration.

## Act I. The Generation of Humanity

Michelangelo's famous fresco in the Sistine Chapel—known as the Finger of God—which depicts the creation of Adam is one of the most famous images in the world. This fresco enhances our understanding of the Christian view of man's spiritual state. God is shown as a bearded man in a swirling cloak next to cherubims. He stretches out his right arm to impart the spark of life from His finger into that of earthbound Adam. Adam's left arm is extended in a pose mirroring God's to show that God created humans in His own image.

> Man enjoyed perfect communion with God in the garden before sin crept into the world.

This touch or communion between God and people continued until Adam and Eve disobeyed God in the garden. As a result, they died spiritually. Their fellowship with the Creator was severed. A great gulf grew between God and humanity. The reason for this gulf is that God is eternally holy and will not allow unholiness in His presence. Because sinning against a just and holy God is an infinite crime, God said that a Savior would bridge this gulf and through suffering, would pay the price for humanity's sin. In essence, Michelangelo's famous fresco of the creation of Adam is the first of three acts in the cycle of life and death.

## Act II. The Degeneration of Humanity

In order to understand the ensuing events after Adam's creation, one must imagine a second fresco. Here's the same painting with the same set of players but with one stark difference—the distance that separates God's finger from Adam's finger.

Adam (and Eve) were now separated from God. Their sin made it

> The distance between God and man grew to infinity because man's sin is a direct assault against God's holiness.

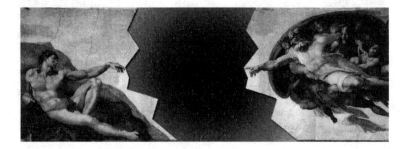

impossible for them to bridge this gulf and have a renewed fellowship with God. It's interesting to note that man still has a finger pointed toward God trying to reach Him through human effort while God has a finger pointed toward man, lovingly longing to reach him through the Messiah at the appointed time.

## Act III. The Regeneration of Humanity

The regeneration of humanity is the third act, but Michelangelo never drew it. Once again, God reaches down from heaven to Adam, and Adam reaches out to God, but this time, two other personalities appear in the picture—the Savior that God promised and the Holy Spirit. The Savior is nailed to a cross, bridging the gap between man's sinfulness and God's holiness. The Savior is touching Adam's finger with His human nature and God's finger with His divine nature.

> The great chasm between Adam (man) and God is now bridged by a Savior covered in blood and crowned with thorns.

The Holy Spirit (on Adam's chest) is also present in the fresco in the form of a dove (Luke 3:22). The work of the Holy Spirit is to convict humans of their

sins and need for repentance. The Bible says that no one can say, "Jesus is Lord," except by the Holy Spirit (1 Cor. 12:3). The Holy Spirit draws humankind to the Father through the Son (Matt. 3:16, 17, Jude 20, 21).

## To Choose or Not to Choose

In countries where the Shari'a (Muslim Jurisprudence) is the law of the land, Muslims are forced to worship during prayer time at the risk of being whipped by the mut-tawa (Islamic morality police). The Shari'a crushes dissent and under-mines most human rights, such as freedom of religion, freedom of expression, political freedoms, and women's rights. It doesn't allow people to choose for themselves, but seeks to enslave them. It's evident that Islam emphasizes the external expression of worship instead of genuine heartfelt praise to the Almighty.

> If worship does not come from the heart, it's a hollow expression meaning nothing to God.

God gives people a choice of whether to live in the second fresco, degeneration—with no hope of fellowshipping with God—or in the third fresco, regeneration—where one's fellowship with God is restored. If God did not allow a human to choose for himself, he would be a puppet. God doesn't want puppets to worship Him because they are forced to, but He wants freewill agents to worship Him from their hearts because they desire to.

## The Incomprehensible Holiness of God

Because the Qur'an states that people are captive to sin (Surah 12:53, 1:5), the logical question is: Can people justify themselves before a holy God? The remaining parts of this chapter will address this dilemma.

When King David was moving the ark of the covenant into Jerusalem on an oxen-driven cart, the oxen stumbled putting the ark in a precarious position. In order to protect the ark from falling, Uzzah touched it. However, God had already commanded the Israelites that only the priests or Levites could touch the ark. As a result, Uzzah committed a capital offense under Hebrew law. So, "The anger of the Lord burned against Uzzah, and God struck him down there for his irreverence; and he died there by the ark of God" (2 Sam. 6:7). It is within that backdrop that King David asked, "Who can dwell before the tabernacle [presence] of the Lord?"

Pastor Jack Graham said that if people believe they can dwell before the tabernacle of the Lord, then they haven't caught a glimpse of the holiness of God. Graham continues:

> We are further from God than we think, and when we real-
> ize how great God is, how powerful, how perfect God is, then
> we'll realize how separated from God we are. And if getting
> to heaven is like climbing some moral ladder, whether in
> achieving or believing, how will I ever know if I've done
> enough? If that is the way that we get to heaven, how could
> we ever know that we've done enough? Somebody said, 'I'll
> just wait 'til I get there and I'll find out.' Well, I don't like
> those kinds of surprises. You can be wrong about your
> income tax statement, you can be wrong about a test, but
> you can't afford to be wrong about this one.[5]

## Islam and the Problem of Sin

Since we know the environment in Eden was not corrupt, we must conclude that Satan brought corruption to Adam and Eve.

But if Adam, as Muslims claim, was the first prophet of Islam, then why didn't his complete submission to Allah uncorrupt him and, thus, repatriate him into paradise? Why was he confined to a life of hardship, work, and sweat, disease, and death? Why weren't his wrongs made right through his submission to Allah? In other words, if Islam works, then why didn't it work for Adam by erasing his sins and repatriating him into paradise? The answer is clear—Islam is flawed. Islam has never addressed the root cause that brought about the Fall within the garden, but simply presented the Muslims with an instruction book on how to live.

One more question: If Muslims are truly born in fitrah (pure state), then why can't they remain pure?

*And if Allah were to destroy men for their iniquity, He would not leave therein a single creature, but He respites them 'til an appointed time. So when their doom comes, they are not able to delay* [it] *an hour, nor can they advance* [it] (Surah 16:61).

The following are logical deductions from the above surah:

• All people are sinners.
• People cannot achieve perfection.
• If God were to judge people for their sins, all would be found guilty.

In order for humans to be in God's presence, they have to be perfect like God, for God cannot allow sin in His presence. God expects absolute moral perfection. It is blasphemy to presume that people can become perfect like God. Muslims who believe in the myth that they can be perfect or atone for their own sins go against their very own scriptures (Surahs 12:53; 16:61). It's interesting to note that the Qur'an claims that only Jesus Christ is sinless (Surah 19:19).

If Islam gravitates toward good, as the Muslims claim, then why is it that in Pakistan, a Muslim country of 140 million, only one million file their tax returns annually? Why are the "basically good" tax evaders prodding Pakistan's government into near bankruptcy and depriving Pakistan's poor of basic government programs? And why do the majority of refugees in the world spill out of Muslim countries?[6] The perceived goodness of Muslims is an illusion.

## Can People Fulfill the Law?

"EDITH LIVED IN A LITTLE WORLD BOUNDED ON
THE NORTH, SOUTH, EAST, AND WEST BY EDITH."[7]

To believe that we are an island unto ourselves is to be self-sufficient, prideful, arrogant, and egotistical like Edith. Edith had no need for God, so she became a god in her own eyes. She set her own boundaries, made her own rules, and crowned herself queen of her world. To believe that we can fulfill the law on our own without God's grace is to exhibit exaggerated pride, blasphemy, and megalomania. If we wish to follow the straight path, we must place our trust in God, not in ourselves, lest we become gods in our own eyes. In contrast, the Muslims believe that by following their pillars of religion, they can attain salvation, which makes God obsolete and makes them a god in their own eyes.

> The Muslims believe that by following their pillars of religion, they can attain salvation, which makes God obsolete and makes them a god in their own eyes.

"It is a well-known dictum among Western Muslims that just as theology occupies the central place in Christianity, in Islam, the central place belongs to the law."[8]

Although the law is verbose and enslaving, it is powerless to justify a person before the Almighty. No matter how many times a beast washes in a river, it remains a beast, and no matter how long a log soaks in the water, it will never become a crocodile. In the same manner, no matter what humankind does in its own strength, they remain sinners in the sight of a holy God.

Like the Qur'an, the Bible counsels us that all of us have sinned:

> Both Jews and Greeks [non-Jews] are all under sin; as it is written, 'There is none righteous, not even one; there is none who understands, there is none who seeks for God; all have turned aside, together they have become useless; there is none who does good, there is not even one. . . . There is no fear of God before their eyes" (Rom. 3:9–12, 18).

In order to take advantage of Jesus' path to the Father, humans must leave behind deceiving notions that they can be perfect like God. The Islamic religion wants us to believe the great lie that we do not need a Savior. Our own sin-stained hands can save us. However, the good news is that salvation is freely available to us through God's grace. Christ is the only way of salvation. No other religion can reconcile us with God except the one that offers a divine Savior.

> Islam wants us to believe the great lie that we do not need a Savior. Our own sin-stained hands can save us.

## The Myth of Small Sin

Jesus told the crowds:

> You have heard that the ancients were told, "You shall not commit murder" and "Whoever commits murder shall be liable to the court." But I say to you that everyone who is angry with his brother shall be guilty before the court; and whoever says to his brother, "You good-for-nothing," shall be guilty before the supreme court; and whoever says, "You fool" shall be guilty enough to go into the fiery hell (Matt. 5:21, 22).

The majority of us consider ourselves to be good people because we subscribe to the myth that there are big sins and small sins. We are misled to believe that if we only commit small sins, such as lying, while abstaining from big sins such as killing, then God will forgive us. However, the Bible makes no distinction between big and small sins. God is not interested in quotas or in the degree of our sin, but He is simply interested in sin. Sin is sin in God's eyes. It cannot be pluralized; it is binary, meaning that we have either sinned or we have not; there is no middle ground or fences to ride. The Ten Commandments confirm God's standard of righteousness. We all have broken these commandments, and all it takes for us to be sinners is to commit one sin.

> God expects absolute moral perfection. The Bible says that if a person commits the smallest sin, then he has become an enemy of God (Rom. 5:6–10).

Since we have all sinned—according to the Bible and the Qur'an—then why should God allow us into heaven and permit unholiness to defile His perfect holiness? Sin is rebellion against the Almighty Himself and since God is not a corrupt judge, He cannot allow sin to go unpunished.

Therefore, our works are impotent in producing forgiveness, because they do not resolve the dilemma of sin. Islam commends people who connect legalistically with religious icons, whether it is washing and praying five times a day, making pilgrimages to Mecca [hajj], fasting [sawm] during Ramadan, or giving alms [zakat] to the poor. Islamic tradition is specific about ritual cleansing in preparation for prayer [salat]. Hence, if Muslims have undergone ablution but come in contact with dirt and then proceed to pray, they are considered unclean and Allah will not accept their prayers. In the same way that dirt makes our bodies unclean, sin makes our souls unclean and disqualifies us from approaching the holy God.

> Therefore, our works are impotent in producing forgiveness, since they do not resolve the dilemma of sin.

The acts of the law, whether praying, fasting, or giving, are all hollow acts in themselves. They are inadequate to cover our sins. I believe the story of Job illustrates this point powerfully.

## Job and the Problem of Sin

Jews, Christians, and Muslims alike revere Job [Ayoub in Arabic]. His name is from the Arabic word meaning "to come back" or "repent." How curious it is that Job had to repent when he was blameless before God and served Him selflessly. Job was morally innocent, according to God's description of him: "There is no one like him on the earth, a blameless and upright man, fearing God and turning away from evil" (Job 1:8). However, Job was subsequently assaulted on every side. He was devastated by the loss of his children, servants, livestock, and home, and he was afflicted with painful sores all over his body.

Why then did Job become the subject of intense suffering physically, spiritually, and emotionally? Is it because Job became proud? Is it because he focused his attention on himself instead of God?

When Job tried to justify himself, the Lord answered him out of a whirlwind and said,

> Who is this that darkens counsel by words without knowledge? Now gird up your loins like a man, and I will ask you, and you instruct Me! "Where were you when I laid the foundation of the earth? Tell Me, if you have understanding, who set its measurements? Since you know. . . .
>
> Have you ever in your life commanded the morning, and caused the dawn to know its place, that it might take hold of the ends of the earth, and the wicked be shaken out of it? . . .
>
> Have the gates of death been revealed to you, or have you seen the gates of deep darkness? . . .
>
> Can you bind the chains of the Pleiades, or loose the cords of Orion? Can you lead forth a constellation in its season, and guide the Bear with her satellites? Do you know the ordinances of the heavens, or fix their rule over the earth? Can you lift up your voice to the clouds, so that an abundance of water will cover you? Can you send forth lightnings that they may go and say to you, "Here we are"? (Job 38:2–5, 12, 13, 17, 31–35).

When God finally spoke to Job out of the mighty storm, Job understood his insignificance before the Almighty, confessed his lack of understanding, and repented from his pride and self-righteousness: "I have heard of You by the hearing of the ear; but now my eye sees You; therefore I retract, and I repent in dust and ashes" (Job 42:5, 6). One glimpse of the holiness of God made Job speechless.

> Then the Lord said to Job, "Will the faultfinder contend with the Almighty? Let him who reproves God answer it." Then Job answered the Lord and said, "Behold, I am insignificant; what can I reply to You? I lay my hand on my mouth" (Job 40:1–4).

Job asked the question of the ages: "How can we be made right with God?" And so, this "blameless and upright man, fearing God and turning away from evil" (Job 1:8) cried out for a redeemer when he understood the holiness of God: "As for me, I know that my Redeemer lives, and at the last He will take His stand on the earth" (Job 19:25). This Redeemer was none other than the Messiah, "The Lamb of God who takes away the sin of the world" (John 1:29).

Pastor Jack Graham points out that all religions underestimate the purity, perfection, and holiness of God and overestimate the righteousness of people. God is holy and perfect. Only the Messiah, whom the Qur'an called perfect (Surah 19:19), is righteous enough to take away the sin of the world.

> **Job understood his insignificance before the Almighty, confessed his lack of understanding, and repented from his self-righteousness.**

## King David and the Problem of Sin

Even King David, who is revered by Jews, Christians, and Muslims alike, cried out in an insightful monologue after his sin against Bathsheba and her husband, "Wash me thoroughly from my iniquity and cleanse me from my sin" (Ps. 51:2). No ordinary man said this. This is King David [Dawood], the man God chose "after His own heart" (1 Sam. 13:14). However, if we are truly born in a pure state as Islam claims, why would this chosen man of God be corrupted by sin? Are even God's prophets slaves to sin?

King David continued, "For I know my transgressions, and my sin is ever before me" (Ps. 51:3). King David does not speak of just one sin, but of perpetual transgressions that do not disappear with his praying, fasting, and pilgrimages. His sin was ever before him and he realized that the Almighty hates sin. David failed to measure up to God's perfect standards. Could this be the human predicament?

King David stated that he was born in sin, thus refuting Islamic claims once and for all, that we are born in a pure state [fitrah]. "Behold, I was brought forth in iniquity, and in sin my mother conceived me" (v. 5). If David, who is considered to be a prophet by Muslims, was plagued with sin, does not this imply that he could never measure up to God's perfect standards on his own no matter how many times he prayed, no matter how many pilgrimages he made, and no matter how many times he circumambulated a shrine—as Muslims do?

David's ensuing request must be troubling to Islam. "Purify me with hyssop, and I shall be clean; wash me, and I shall be whiter than snow" (v. 7). After all, Islam preaches a doctrine of legalism with prescribed prayers and pillars that believers must follow to be justified by the Almighty. If all the Judeo-Christian prophets were Muslims and surrendered to the will of Allah, as

Islam claims, then David must have had it within himself to atone for his own sins instead of asking God to cleanse him. David must have known, as all Muslims know, that God does not atone, wash, or cleanse sins, for people can do this themselves. But, contrary to Islamic assertions, David asked God to purify him with hyssop. Hyssop was used on the Jewish Day of Atonement to sprinkle blood during priestly ceremonies. Why did David ask God to purify him with blood when Muslims consider him one of their holy prophets, as one surrendered to the complete will of Allah? Could it be because he realized he was unclean in the sight of the Almighty and his works would never wash away sin?

David continued, "Hide Your face from my sins and blot out all my iniquities" (v. 9). God is a God of order and our sins introduce chaos into His perfect order. Isaiah gives us helpful insights into the effects of sin that David asked God to hide His face from: "But your iniquities have made a separation between you and your God, and your sins have hidden His face from you so that He does not hear" (59:2). David therefore asked God to bridge the gap that his sin created between himself and a holy God. David could not resolve this separation and therefore he asked God to intervene. This is a hint of Christ's later intervention on our behalf, when God did for us what we could never do for ourselves. Isn't it blasphemous for Muslims to believe that unlike David, they can blot out their sins with their dead works without God's divine intervention?

The Islamic scholar, Abdul Saleeb, points to a troubling aspect concerning the Qur'an. He states that in the entire Qur'an, the word "holy" is only attributed to God twice (Surahs 59:23 and 62:1). Though God's portrayal in the Qur'an is in majestic and sovereign terms, a single verse in the Bible (Isa. 6:3) has more references (three) to the holiness of God than the whole of the Islamic scriptures.[9] Saleeb asserts that because only two passages refer to the holiness of Allah in the Qur'an, this fact has shaped the limited Muslim understanding of how holy God is. Saleeb states: "Because of that understanding of God, and the diminished view of how holy He is, it is obviously very hard for Muslims to understand how sinful we are, and the radical nature of human sinfulness."[10]

## Summary

Muslims believe that their acts will be weighed on the great scales of justice. If the good deeds outweigh the bad, they will go to heaven instead of hell. The problem in this thinking is how can a person know for sure that he is moral, righteous, pure, or good enough? How could one ever cut through the fears and uncertainty and know beyond the shadow of a doubt that he has performed enough? Salvation is not about achieving, but it's about believing that the Savior offers the unmerited gift of grace from the Father, a gift which costs a person nothing but which cost the Son of God everything. Such is the incomprehensible love of God.

# THREE

# Is the Qur'an the True Word of God?

*The Qur'an is "an incoherent rhapsody of fable, and precept, and declamation, which sometimes crawls in the dust, and sometimes is lost in the clouds."*

—EDWARD GIBBON

## Genesis of the Qur'an

Muslims believe that their holy book, the Qur'an, is eternal having always existed on eternal stone tablets in heaven. They believe that the current copy of the Qur'an is identical to the one found in heaven because Allah does not allow his word to be altered. But to critically investigate the sources and development of the religious ideas expounded in the Qur'an is blasphemous to a Muslim.[1] The late Islamic scholar Alfred Guillaume rationalized this view by describing the Qur'an as the Muslims' "holy of holies." Consequently, Muslims are taught to accept their canons without the benefit of rational inquiry or scientific examination. It is not surprising, therefore, that Islamic scholars, such as Arthur Jeffery, describe the critical investigation of the Qur'an as being still in its infancy. Decades after Jeffery, scholar John Wansbrough also pointed out that by the rigorous standards of instruments and techniques used in biblical criticism, the Qur'an is virtually unknown. Years later, scholar Andrew Rippin lamented the lack of critical thought in the introductory books of Islam.[2] In stark contrast to the Qur'an, the Bible has been subjected to the most rigorous principles of scientific inquiry and has been substantiated by countless archeological discoveries.

> Muslims are taught to accept their canons without the benefit of rational inquiry or scientific examination.

Although modern Muslims assert that the Qur'an used today is identical to that recited by Islam's prophet, earlier Muslims were more realistic. They realized that much of the Qur'an was lost and the thousands of variants made it impossible to speak of "the Qur'an."[3] Abu 'Ubaid al-Qasim b. Sallam (AH 154–244 [After Hijra]), who studied under the famous masters of the Qufan and Basran schools, was renowned as a philologist, a jurist, and an authority on the Qur'anic sciences included in *Kitab Fada'il-al-Qur'an* (folios 43 and 44), an entire chapter on the verses that have fallen out of the Qur'an. The most famous of those verses concerned Omar who admitted that much of the Qur'an had been lost. Aisha, the prophet's favorite wife, asserted along with Ubai Ibn Ka'b, one of Muhammad's closest companions, that the chapter of the parties (Surah 33) had at one time contained two hundred verses. Aisha even claimed that Uthman altered the codices.[4]

Even the Muslim caliphs, Omar B. Al-Khattab and Uthman, refer to the missing verses in the Qur'an concerning the account of the stoning of the adulterers reported in the Ahadith. In addition, Abu Waqid Al-Laithi, Musa al-Ashari, Zaid b. Arqam, and Jabir bin Abdallah all spoke of verses that the prophet Muhammad often repeated concerning human greed—"if Adam's son had two valleys of gold, he would desire a third." It's reported that Omar sent Abd ar-Rahman b. Auf to look in the Qur'an for these verses that had been revealed. When unable to find the missing verses, Abd ar-Rahman answered, "It dropped out among what dropped from the Qur'an."[5]

According to author Arthur Jeffery, many variants existed, even of the fatiha (Surah 1) of the Qur'an, including one in the book Tadhkirat al-A'imma (by Muhammad Baquir Majlisi) and another in the little manual of Fikh. In addition, Khalil Ahmad, the reader from the famous Basran school, had yet another variant of the fatiha (Surah 1). Ahmad transmitted variants from Isa b. Omar (AH 149 or AD 766) and was a pupil of Ayyub as-Sakhtiyani (AH 131 or AD 748), both of whom were famous for their transmission of uncanonical variants. However, if verses were dropped out of the Qur'an, it's also true that other verses were added, for the earliest Muslim commentators (e.g., Abu Bakr al Asamm, AH 313 or AD 925) openly attacked the fatiha as uncanonical.[6]

The Qur'anic variants were preserved by commentaries of numerous Muslim scholars during the early days of Islam. However, Muslim scholars have not attempted a textual criticism

> Although modern Muslims assert that the Qur'an used today is identical to that recited by Islam's prophet, earlier Muslims were more realistic.

> When unable to find the missing verses (in the Qur'an), Abd ar-Rahman answered, "It dropped out among what dropped from the Qur'an."

of the Qur'an since AH 322 (AD 934) when the canons were fixed by Wazirs Ibn Muqla and Ibn Isa, assisted by Ibn Mujahid. Those who persisted in using variant texts of the Qur'an, such as Ibn Miqsam (AH 362 or AD 972) and Ibn

> Not only did verses drop out of the Qur'an, but verses were also added.

Shanabudh, were severely punished in order to bring an end to variant readings. The variations are preserved, however, in the Qur'an commentaries of az-Zamakhshari (AH 538 or AD 1143), Abyu Hayyan of Andalus (AH 745 or AD 1344), and Ash-Shakawani (AH 1250 or AD 1834); and in the philological works of al-Ukbari (AH 616 or AD 1219), the philosopher of Baghdad, Ibn Khalawaih (AH 370 or AD 980), the savant of the Hamdanid Court, and the famous scholar Ibn Jinni (AH 392 or AD 1001).[7]

Approximately forty years before Bukhari (the compiler of the most famous collection of Ahadith by the title of Sahih Bukhari), Al Kindy (AD 830), who served at the court of the caliph Al Ma'mum, documented the history of the Qur'an as follows: Upon the death of the prophet Muhammad, Ali, who wanted to succeed to the caliphate, delayed in swearing allegiance to Abu Bakr, successor to the prophet. When Ali finally presented himself before Abu Bakr, Ali claimed that he was delayed because the prophet had entrusted collecting the Qur'an into his care. Eventually, Ali presented to Abu Bakr the Qur'an that had been collected from the memory of individuals, tablets of stone, palm leaves, and shoulder bones. Because the Qur'an was not collected in a volume but remained in separate leaves, there were many canonical variations. Some people read the version of Ali, while others read the text of Ibn Mas'ud, Ubai Ibn Ka'b, or countless others.[8] Therefore, to claim that the Qur'an is unchanged is a grave historical error. Because the Qur'an was changed, then its' origins could not have been divine, for God would have protected it.

> To claim that the Qur'an is unchanged is a grave historical error.

Moreover, Al Kindy recounts that when Uthman became caliph, "One man would read a verse one way, and another man another way; and there was change and interpolation, some copies having more and some less." Uthman then saw the danger of division, strife, and apostasy as a result of having a variety of codices, so he had Zaid Ibn Thabit and Abdallah Ibn Abbas collect all the leaves and scraps of the Qur'an in order to standardize it. After revising and correcting the various texts, and the revision was completed, Uthman had all the copies of the Qur'an burned except his codex. (It is apparent, however, that Ali's codex survived along with other scattered variants.) Four copies of Uthman's codex were, subsequently, made on scrolls of parchment [suhufs] and sent to different Muslim provinces. Years later, under the caliphate of 'Abdul-Malik (684–704), Hajjaj b. Yusuf gathered all the copies of the Qur'an, changed passages as he wished, and destroyed the others as Uthman had previously done. He made six copies of the new version and sent them out to various Muslim provinces. Al Kindy concludes: "The enmity subsisting between Ali and Abu Bakr, Omar and Uthman is well known; now each of these caliphs entered in the text whatever favored his own claims, and left out what was otherwise. How, then, can we distinguish between the genuine and the counterfeit?"[9]

> The enmity subsisting between Ali and Abu Bakr, Omar and Uthman is well known; now each of these entered in the text whatever favored his own claims, and left out what was otherwise. How, then, can we distinguish between the genuine and the counterfeit? —Al Kindy

Therefore, we must put away the notion that the Qur'an was available from a single source. The evidence clearly shows us that the Qur'an was birthed and amalgamated through a laborious process of discovery, scrutiny, and investigation. Alphonse Mingana, the great scholar of Semitic languages, points out that Ibn Thabit probably tried to faithfully reproduce the words of the prophet Muhammad. If not, he would have attempted to improve the style and grammar and amend the historical and typographical errors. Mingana dubs the Muslim claim that the Qur'an is perfect Arabic as absurd due to the many examples of repetition, weak rhyme, changing letters to force a rhyme, foreign words, and bizarre usage or change of names (e.g., John to Yahwa, Jesus to 'Isa, Elijah to Yasa, Terah to Azar, Saul to Talut, and Enoch to Idris).[10]

The Qur'an was essentially birthed and amalgamated through a laborious process of discovery, scrutiny, and investigation.

The Ahadith tell us that Abu Bakr was the first to collate the texts of the Qur'an into a single codex, and he passed it down to Omar and then to Hafsa. According to tradition, Zaid Ibn Thabit wrote the Qur'an at least twice—once under Abu Bakr and another under Uthman. In order to assemble the Qur'an, Ibn Thabit relied on texts from the memory of Arabs as well as scattered scraps of parchments, prior to engaging in a laborious study of standardizing the canons.[11] But if no variant read-

> **Why did Uthman burn other copies of the Qur'an if they were all similar?**

ings existed as some Muslims assert, then why did Ibn Thabit embark on the same work twice? And why did Uthman burn other copies of the Qur'an if they were all similar?

Even the Ahadith confirmed that Uthman ordered all variant copies of the Qur'an to be burned.[12] In fact, the early Muslim scholars, Tabari and Yakut, separately documented that Uthman was called the "Tearer of the Books," thus confirming that there were many variants to the Qur'an. The alarmed Muslim popu-lace attached to Uthman the following stigma: "He found the Qur'ans many and left one; he tore up the Book."[13] The canonical differences of the text, however, could not have been restricted to

vowelizing (furnishing with vowels— Arabic accents/markings to make the text more readable), as some Muslims claim. The orientalist Alphonse Mingana documented that there is no manuscript from before the latter half of the eighth

> **Uthman was called the "Tearer of the Books."**

century that is adorned with vowels, as vowels were not yet incor-porated into the Arabic script from the Arameans.[14]

Since vowels (accents/markings) were not yet used in the Arabic language, the differences between the variant texts could not have been restricted to vowels. These differences between the

Qur'anic variants must have been large and meaningful enough to show up even in the primitive texts. Since the Arabic script was not fully developed when the Qur'an was assembled, it's inconceivable that the Qur'an, revealed by Islam's prophet and written down in part during his life, was identical to a Qur'an that existed in Arabic on a preserved tablet in heaven. Unfortunately, we will never know the full extent of the variants since Uthman conveniently burned the evidence.[15] One thing is certain, however: the Qur'an revealed to Islam's prophet is not eternal, nor did it survive unchanged throughout the centuries.

> **The Qur'an revealed to Islam's prophet is not eternal, nor did it survive unchanged throughout the centuries.**

Muslims often argue that two of the four original copies of the Uthmanic version are still available, one in the Topkapi Museum in Istanbul and one in Tashkent, Uzbekistan. Most serious scholars, however, date those to the ninth century. In fact, many non-Muslim scholars hold the Ma'il copy in the British Library to be the oldest, most complete copy of the modern Qur'an. It was dated AD 790, 158 years after the prophet's death. Recent work on Qur'anic manuscripts discovered in Sana'a, Yemen, proved that the Qur'an has evolved considerably since the time of Uthman and it has continued to evolve. This is evidenced by whole sections that have come

> **Over one thousand variants of the Qur'anic text have been found within the first eighty-three surahs alone.**

up missing or have been added by a later hand, such as passages that read today as "say" (a divine command to the prophet Muhammad), which are seen to have once been: "he said . . ." or "they said . . ." These two phrases seem to indicate the attributing of human words to Allah. In addition over one thousand variants have been found within the first eighty-three surahs alone.[16]

> Caliph Al Ma'moun ridiculed the idea that the Qur'an was uncreated.

Thus, the power struggle for the caliphate, greatly prejudiced the development of the Qur'an, as well as the expansion of Islamic canons by countless ambitious Muslims who guaranteed themselves high positions and prestige by producing Ahadith. For that reason, instead of having always existed as Muslims claim, the Qur'anic text has evolved and been standardized over time. Ample evidence that the Qur'an has evolved prompted the caliph Al Ma'moun (AD 786–833) to issue his famous edict denying the eternal existence of the Qur'an.[17] In fact, Al Ma'moun ridiculed the idea that the Qur'an was uncreated.[18]

The Mu'tazilites argued during the rule of the Abbasid Khalifate that the Qur'an was created, citing Surah 43:3. Clinton Bennett rightly points out: "If the Qur'an is uncreated, this risks a duality, associating a partner with God."[19]

> If the Qur'an is uncreated, this risks a duality, associating a partner with God.
> —Clinton Bennett

## A Critical Analysis of the Angel Gabriel

While analyzing the genesis of the Qur'an, I would be remiss if I failed to mention the role of the angel Gabriel in the Qur'anic revelations. Muslims regard the Qur'an as the word of Allah given to the prophet Muhammad by a piecemeal process (Surah 76:23) by sending down revelations [tanzil]. The mediator between Allah and the prophet Muhammad, who revealed the Qur'an to him, was at times called the "Spirit" (Surah 19:17), the "Holy Spirit" (Surah 16:102), "Gabriel" (Surah 2:97), or an angel (Surah 3:44).

In the folklore of Islam, Jibra'il (the angel Gabriel) was the voice that revealed to the prophet Muhammad that he was chosen to be God's messenger. Gabriel supposedly revealed the Qur'an to the prophet Muhammad over a span of twenty-three years and appeared to the prophet in physical form on two occasions. The first of these was at the Mountain of Light at the beginning of the revelations, and the second at the prophet's ascension [mir'aj]. Gabriel is portrayed in the Qur'an as the protector of the prophet (Surah 66:4) despite the fact that Gabriel was notably absent when Islam's prophet needed protection. (He was on various occasions pelted with stones, struck with the sword on his face, poisoned, etc.)

It's interesting to note that Islam's prophet is styled in the Qur'an as a prophet in the tradition of Moses. Moses, however, received the Ten Commandments from God Himself in the midst of publicly manifested miraculous signs and wonders instead of at the hands of an angel. The Jews of the day must have drawn these comparisons between Moses and Muhammad. If one is to accept that Gabriel was the mediator, he is left with a quandary of epic proportion, for the angel Gabriel in the Qur'an is in total contradiction to both Gabriel's mission and identity in the Bible.

Gabriel was introduced in the book of Daniel at which time he gave the prophet Daniel an understanding of his vision of the end times (8:16–26). At the heart of that vision was the King of kings— the Messiah. Gabriel reappears in the following chapter to give

Daniel the exact date of the triumphal entry of the Messiah into
Jerusalem, five centuries before the
actual birth of Christ:

> Seventy weeks have been decreed
> for your people and your holy
> city, to finish the transgression,
> to make an end of sin, to make
> atonement for iniquity, to bring
> in everlasting righteousness, to
> seal up vision and prophecy and
> to anoint the most holy place
> (Dan. 9:24).

> **The Bible demonstrates that the angel Gabriel had a single unwavering mission—to announce the coming of the Messiah, the Savior of the world.**

Sixty-nine weeks of seven years (69x7) equals 483 years, leading up to March 30, AD 33, the exact date of the actual triumphal
entry of Jesus Christ into Jerusalem.[20]

This same Gabriel appeared, again, to Mary to announce the
coming birth of Jesus Christ six centuries before the prophet
Muhammad:[21]

> And behold, you will conceive in your womb and bear a son,
> and you shall name Him Jesus. He will be great and will be
> called the Son of the Most High; and the Lord God will give
> Him the throne of His father David; and He will reign over
> the house of Jacob forever, and His kingdom will have no
> end (Luke 1:31–33).

The angel Gabriel also appeared to Zacharias to announce the
birth of John the Baptist, the forerunner of the Messiah:

"It is he [John the Baptist] who will go as a forerunner before Him in the spirit and power of Elijah, to turn the hearts of the fathers back to the children, and the disobedient to the attitude of the righteous, so as to make ready a people prepared for the Lord." Zacharias said to the angel, "How will I know this for certain? For I am an old man and my wife is advanced in years." The angel answered and said to him, "I am Gabriel, who stands in the presence of God, and I have been sent to speak to you and to bring you this good news (Luke 1:17–19).

Again, the angel of the Lord[22] appeared to Joseph, saying:

"Joseph, son of David, do not be afraid to take Mary as your wife; for the Child who has been conceived in her is of the Holy Spirit. She will bear a Son; and you shall call His name Jesus, for He will save His people from their sins." Now all this took place to fulfill what was spoken by the Lord through the prophet: "Behold, the virgin shall be with Child and shall bear a Son, and they shall call His name Immanuel," which translated means, "God with us" (Matt. 1:20–23).

Thus, we repeatedly find in the Biblical narrative that Gabriel, "who stands in the presence of God," was sent by God with a single mission. Gabriel's mission throughout the Bible was to announce the coming

> **It is absurd for Gabriel to announce a contradictory gospel, since it would cast shadows on God's unchanging character.**

of the Messiah, the only Savior, Redeemer, and Son of the Most High God. It's absurd for Gabriel to announce a contradictory gospel, since it would cast shadows on God's unchanging character. God does not make mistakes, for His plans are perfect.

Islam's superficial understanding concerning the biblical Scriptures is clearly manifested when the Qur'an insinuates that Gabriel and the Holy Spirit are one: *"Say, the Holy Spirit has brought the revelation from your Lord in truth"* (Surah 16:102).

In another verse (Surah 2:97), we learn that Gabriel purportedly brought down the revelation. The implication that the angel Gabriel and the Holy Spirit are the same is troubling. It's a gross misunderstanding of God to claim that Gabriel, a created being, is the Holy Spirit of God, or God Himself. It's no wonder that Jews ridiculed the idea that Gabriel brought revelation to the prophet Muhammad (Surah 2:97, 98).

> It's a gross misunderstanding of God to claim that Gabriel, a created being, is the Holy Spirit of God, or God Himself.

Another major disparity between the angel Gabriel as depicted in the Bible and as depicted in the Qur'an is that the biblical Gabriel appeared to many personalities while executing his mission of announcing the Messiah. The Qur'anic Gabriel, on the other hand, appeared only to one man while delivering the Qur'an—the prophet Muhammad. This clandestine protocol is the blueprint of the Qur'an. The wonders of the sending down of the Qur'anic revelations [tanzil] seem to be restricted from the masses and shrouded in an aura of stealth and mystery like some governmental underground operation or a secret society, but boasted of only one member. In Islam, there are no witnesses to Gabriel or his miracles. There are no forerunners to the prophet announcing his coming and confirming his message. The revelations seem to have occurred in a vacuum of time and space with only one set of eyes—the prophet Muhammad.

In a modern court, if the defendant and the judge were the same, the trial would be considered a mockery. If Islam were on trial during its early years, the prophet of Islam would have had no witnesses to testify of his angelic visitations or his night trips to Jerusalem during his heavenly voyage [mi'raj] on the back of a human-faced donkey-mule.[23] The issues behind this mysterious concealment are in stark contrast to the openness of the Bible in which God's signs and wonders were performed in public.

With the Qur'an, in contrast to God's intervention, there was no manna falling from the sky. There was no star leading the Magi to the long-awaited Savior. There was no angel announcing the birth of Islam's founder to shepherds. There was no voice of God speaking from the heavens as when Jesus was being baptized. There was no darkness filling the earth or people rising from the dead when Islam's prophet died. This leads us to ask—

> Are we to believe that God made a mistake in sending Gabriel as the announcer of the Messiah and later resent Gabriel with a contradictory message?

has God changed? Has the Creator suddenly lost His powers? Or did He become a stealth god? God has not changed. He is from everlasting to everlasting. He is true to His character and is eternally perfect.

## Sources of Islam

Islam was heavily influenced by many external sources including the hanifs, Jews, and Christians. Many diverse practices and beliefs were infused into the Qur'an and the Islam way of life. The Ahadith inform us that Islam adopted the pagan tradition of kissing the black stone in the Ka'aba (place of worship). St. Clair-Tisdall, the brilliant linguist who researched the sources of Islam in their original languages, summarizes the serious implications of this borrowing: "If we can trace the teaching of the Qur'an or any part of it, to an earthly source, or to human systems existing previous to the prophet's age, then Islam at once falls to the ground."[24]

> If we can trace the teaching of the Qur'an or any part of it, to an earthly source, or to human systems existing previous to the prophet's age, then Islam at once falls to the ground.
> —St. Clair-Tisdall

Ibrahim (Abraham) was renown in Arabia as a worshiper of the one true God. Men known as hanifs arose in Mecca, Medina, and Taif who lamented the evil ways of their people and called for a return to the worship of the one true God, the God of Abraham. The hanifs were disgusted by the Arabs' evil ways, including worshiping idols, eating carrion (flesh unfit as food), drinking blood, sacrificing animals to idols, and putting their newborn daughters to death. Four hanifs were in Mecca, according to Zohry (AH 12 or AD 633) and his pupil Ibn Ishaq (AH 151 or AD 768), from which we have the following account in the Sirat Ibn Hisham (AH 213 or AD 828).

During a pagan Eed (religious holiday), as the Quraish (tribe of Islam's prophet) were slaying the sacrifices and making circuits around the Ka'aba (place of worship), four friends—Waraqa son of Naufal, Ubaidallah son of Jahsh, 'Uthman son of Huwayrith, and Zaid son of Amr—spoke and said: "By the Lord, our people have nothing left of the faith of Abraham. What is this stone that we should encircle it? It can neither hear nor speak, neither hurt nor help. O our people! Look out for your souls, for by the Lord ye are altogether wanting."

> **What is this stone that we should encircle it? It can neither hear nor speak, neither hurt nor help.**
> **—Zaid son of Amr the Hanif**

These hanifs then separated and departed into various lands in search of the faith of Abraham. Waraqa became a Nestorian Christian; Ubaidallah embraced Islam after awhile, and then became a Christian; 'Uthman embraced the Christian faith in Byzantium; and Zaid broke off from the pagan practices of his people, prayed for forgiveness of his sins, worshiped the God of Abraham, and was expelled by Islam's prophet from Mecca to Mount Hira as a result. According to one Hadith, Zaid used to tell the people of Quraish:

"O people of Quraish! By Allah, none amongst you is on the religion of Abraham except me" (*Sahih Bukhari*, vol. 5, bk. 58, no. 169).

Although these four Meccan hanifs were related to Muhammad, none of them embraced Islam. Their teachings had an indelible impact and influence on Islam. These teachings included doctrines about the unity of God, refraining from idol worship, refraining from burying of infant daughters, the doctrines of paradise and hell, and calling God Al Rahman Al Raheem ["the Lord most Merciful and Compassionate"],[25] which the Qur'an copied. In fact, Shakir's translation of the Qur'an includes a direct reference to the hanifs: *"And they say: Be Jews or Christians, you will be on the right course. Say: Nay!* [we follow] *the religion of Ibrahim, the hanif, and he was not one of the polytheists"* (Surah 2:135)[26] (see also Surah 3:67, 95; 4:125; 6:161; 16:120, 123).

The Qur'an had a very high regard for Ibrahim. In fact, Ibrahim is mentioned sixty-three times in the surahs. In eight of those surahs, he is referred to as "Hanif." It was important for Muhammad to be recognized by the Jews as a prophet in order to give legitimacy to the Qur'anic revelations. He recognized that the Jews were the true guardians of the religion of Ibrahim. Thus, Islam's prophet freely adopted countless stories from the Bible in an effort to court and appease the Jews. Tracing the evolution of the prophet's relationship with the Jews provides us with some insights into the changing character of the Islamic Allah.

Islam's prophet attempted to appeal to the "people of the Book" (Christians and Jews) as the bearers of the religion of Abraham. He wanted to tear down the walls that separated the monotheists in order to create a "universal" hanifite religion. In fact, historical records claim that early Muslims were known as hanifs. Nevertheless, as the religiously influential and powerful Jews rejected Islam, the prophet grew impatient with them, so he slaughtered some of them and exiled them from the land (see Surah 5:33).

The prophet's attitude toward the Jews over the years changed. It went from the extreme of reaching out to them in the Qur'an to ordering their slaughter in the same Qur'an. W. St. Clair Tisdall summarizes this affair:

And so we learn from these successive passages in the Qur'an, that the great and unchanging Almighty God, step by step, allowed his divine law to be altered as the prophet and his followers gradually gained successive victories by the sword. Not only so, but we see the same liberty of change permitted in respect of certain passages in the Qur'an to be cancelled by other passages; thus in Surah 2:106: "We abrogate no verse, or cause it to be left out, but we bring in its place a better, or one like unto it. Ah! Dost thou not know that God is over all things almighty?"[27]

Longing for a universal faith, Islam's prophet was happy to accommodate a myriad of sources into the Qur'an, including imaginary and childish tales along with elements that were not associated with Ibrahim. Some of the Qur'anic sources include:

- *Pagan poetry:* Two passages from the Sabaa Mu'allaqat of Imra'ul Qays, which used to hang from the Ka'aba, are quoted in the Qur'an (Surahs 21:96; 29:31, 46; 37:69; 54:1; 93:1). In one Hadith, Imra'ul's daughter mocks Fatima, Muhammad's daughter, because her father is plagiarizing him and claiming to be quoting revelation.[28] The daughter of Imra'ul was subsequently eliminated.
- *Sabeans:* This pagan religious group that worshiped the starry hosts has now disappeared. Even so, the following Sabean customs have been incorporated into Islam:[29]
  - Seven daily prayers, five of them at the same times as those chosen by Islam
  - Praying for the dead
  - Fasting thirty days from night to sunrise

- Observing Eed (religious festivities)
- Venerating the Ka'aba
- *Other pagan cults:* In Islam, the angel Malik rules over hell [Jehennam], a name taken from Molech, who was worshiped as the ruler of fire by ancient idolaters in Palestine.[30] Allah was also worshiped as the moon god throughout the region with the crescent moon as his symbol prior to the advent of Islam.
- *Arabian fables:* The Qur'an retold pre-Islamic folktales as if they were true. These included legends about:
  - Jinns (spirits) (Surahs 15:27; 55:15; 55:33; 72:1);
  - A story of a she-camel who leapt out of a rock to become a prophetess (Surahs 7:73, 77; 54:27–29; 91:13–14);
  - The story of a Jewish village whose people God turned into apes because they broke the Sabbath by fishing (Surah 2:65; 7:163–166);
  - The fable of four dead, cut-up birds that flew (Surah 2:260).[31]
- *Eastern religions:* The Qur'an and Ahadith include many stories borrowed from the Zoroastrian and Hindu religions of the East. These include:
  - The night of power (mir'aj) when Muhammad purportedly traveled through the seven heavens;
  - The seventy-two virgin mermaids of paradise to fulfill every jihadist's desire;
  - Azazil and other spirits coming from Hades;
  - The "light" of Muhammad;
  - The bridge of Sirat;
  - Paradise with its pleasures of women, wine, and songs;
  - The king of death;
  - The peacock story.[32]

- **Heathen Arabic customs:** Local customs in vogue among the heathen were retained in Islam, such as family restrictions in marriage, a hajj to Mecca (pilgrimage), along with circumambulation, visiting Saga and Marwa, throwing stones at the devil in Wadi Mina, ablution (ceremonial cleansing prior to prayers), and kissing the black stone in the Ka'aba.[33]
- **Judaism:** Surah 21:105 is a direct quotation of Psalm 37:11 in the Bible. How could the Qur'an quote the Psalms unless it came after them? Either the Psalms must be eternal or the Qur'an is not.[34] The Qur'an is littered with stories from the Jewish Talmud, the Midrash, and other apocryphal works, including the *Protevangelion's James the Lesser* (used in Surah 3:35–37); the *Testament of Abraham* (used in Surah 87:19); Pirke Rabbi Eleazer; the *Targum of Jonathan ben Uzziah*; the *Targum of Jerusalem* (used in Surah 5:30, 31); and the *Midrash Yalkut* (Surah 2:102).[35]
- **Heretical Christianity:** Islam's conception of Christianity came through its gnostic and heretical forms. According to *The Encyclopedia Britannica*, the gospel was known to Islam's prophet chiefly through apocryphal and heretical sources.[36] This includes Coptic stories from the *Gospel of St. Thomas*, which the prophet must have heard from Myriam, his Coptic concubine. Stories such as baby Jesus speaking from the cradle (Surah 3:46; 19:29–33) and making a bird from clay (Surah 3:49; 5:110) found their way into Islam.[37] Other non-biblical heretical stories, which made their way into the Qur'an, include mistaking the Holy Trinity to represent God, Mary (instead of the Holy Spirit), and Jesus (Surah 5:116) (as if to imply a sexual union between God and Mary to produce Jesus), believing that Jesus did not die on the

cross (Surah 4:157), as well as the story of the seven sleepers (Surah 18:9–26). All these deviating tales existed hundreds of years before the advent of Islam. The Qur'an freely copied them.

When I visited Lebanon several years ago, I went to the mountains to bask in the majesty of the great biblical cedars of Lebanon. While there, I frequented tourist kiosks to find novelty items to bring back to the States. Small Phoenician figurines caught my attention. It was a group of bronze, votive statues 16 cm in height with long pointed hats covered with gold leaves. I knew that these figurines were similar to ones found in the temple of the obelisks and in the tombs of the rulers of biblical Byblos dating back to the eighteenth century BC. I was tempted to buy these statuettes for my office as novelty items to remind me of my country's rich Phoenician heritage, however, my spirit became ill at ease. I knew these statuettes were Phoenician idols. *Why should I bring a curse upon myself?* I thought. I knew that if something has even the appearance of evil, then it is evil. The Bible cautions us to "abstain from every form of evil" (1 Thess. 5:22). As a result, I resisted purchasing those seemingly innocent figurines.

Since then, I've wondered: If Islam came from the Creator, why would it embrace pagan, animistic practices, such as kissing a black stone, encircling the Ka'aba on pilgrimages, or making the Ka'aba (a pagan relic) the object of prayer? Why would Islam focus the Muslims' attention on things rather than on the Creator?

I can only conclude that since the Qur'an contains material from many sources such as pagan, heretical Christian, heathen, cultic, poetic, and from fables, then the notion that Islam is heavenly in origin is intellectually embarrassing!

## Rational Inquiry of the Qur'an

Meccans took issue with the prophet's message and did not believe it but demanded a miracle of him. Because the prophet could not produce a miracle, he pointed with boldness and self-confidence to the Qur'an as an evidential miracle. Al Kindy states: "The truth, in short, is that the Qur'an with its manifold defects could only have appeared a miracle of eloquence and learning in the eyes of rude ignorant tribes and barbarous races."[38] Apparently, Meccans were learned, and thus remained unimpressed, except for a small band of disenfranchised people who joined the prophet's Islam: "He gained them over by yielding to their national love of raids and forays, such as that against the caravan belonging to Abu Jahl; and it was this which led to the prophet leaving Mecca after a ministry of thirteen years with only forty followers."[39]

As a result, the prophet and his small band of followers later immigrated to Medina where Islam gained many adherents. People joined, not by the so-called miracle of the Qur'an, but "some by fear and the sword, some tempted by power and wealth, others drawn by the lusts and pleasures of this life."[40] Years later, after the prophet became powerful in Medina, he overran Mecca with his army and instituted forcible conversions, which became the hallmark of Islam during its formative years. Thus, for the first time in history, the worship of God was enforced by the sword.

## The Two Islams

Muslim scholars divide the Qur'an into two distinct sections, Meccan and Medinan revelations. Like Charles

> For the first time in history, the worship of God was enforced by the sword.

Dickens's *Tale of Two Cities*, these two distinct divisions are opposites, and at odds with one another. They reveal two different Islams with two conflicting value systems. The tacit mantras of these two Islams are:

- Meccan Islam—is to "live and let live"
- Medinan Islam—is to "believe as I do or die."

These two Islams are as far removed from one another as far as the East is removed from the West. They compete against one another in the hearts and minds of Muslims everywhere. Yet the irony of ironies is that they derive their respective doctrines from the same Qur'an. Thus, when the casual Western observer asks "Is Islam a religion of peace or terror?," the answer is both.

*Meccan Islam.* The first Islam was birthed during the first thirteen years of Muhammad's ministry and is often referred to as Pre-Hijra (emigration). The Qur'anic revelations for this Islam took place in Muhammad's hometown of Mecca. Islam failed to gain a large following during this period as Muslims suffered from discrimination and harassment by the local population. Eventually, Muslims emigrated to Medina, and were soon followed by Islam's prophet. The revelations during this period appear to be under the Christian influence, encouraging peace and tolerance. The use of violence was forbidden, even in cases of self-defense. This Islam was the basis for the mystical Sufi movement. The following verse encapsulates the tolerance of this Islam:[41]

*Those who believe [in the Qur'an], and those who follow the Jewish [Scriptures], and the Christians and the Sabians, any who believe in Allah and the Last Day and work righteousness, shall have their reward with their Lord; on them shall be no fear, nor shall they grieve* (Surah 2:62).

The iconic symbol of this Islam is best represented by the Islamic Golden Age (AD 750–1200). Scientific and intellectual achievements which blossomed during this period contributed widely to the Age of the Renaissance in the West. Unlike today's Madrassas (Islamic religious schools) whose education consists of only teaching and memorizing the Qur'an, this Islam was enabled by tolerance and openness to external ideas, such as Greek philosophy and the Eastern concept of zero (believed to have come from India). It welcomed external thoughts, inventions, and innovations, and built upon them.

**During the early days of Islam, Meccan Islam encouraged peace and tolerance.**

Some critics argue that the Islamic Golden Age flourished despite Islam, not because of it. This is due to the fact that persecution, death, or exile were meted out to philosophers whose writings did not conform to the canon such as Ibn Rushd (Averroës) who attempted to reconcile Aristotle's writings into Islam and was banished for a period as a result. Nevertheless, even though the Golden Age of Islam was not perfect, it contributed enormously to technology, sciences, medicine, arts, and philosophy due to an openness to external ideas and influences. Meccan Islam ushered advancement and progress. It is characterized by a less rigid interpretation of the canons and is more tolerant to freedom of expression.

*Medinan Islam.* The second Islam is a jihadist Islam. It occurred when Muhammad emigrated (Post-Hijra) to Medina, and it marks Islam's growth era. To justify the earlier pacifist passages from Mecca, Islam's prophet told his adherents that jihad (holy war) is permissible to those who are wronged (Surah 22:39). Thus, since Muhammad was forced out of Mecca, defensive Jihad was justified to enable his return. This Islam is bent on the destruction of anything that does not follow or support it. It is an archenemy of the West. It leaves no room for dialogue or freedom of expression, but it mercilessly crushes dissent. Sheikh Abed Al-Qadr Bin Abed Al-Aziz (real name is Al-Sayed Imam Al-Aziz Al-Sharif) is the spiritual mentor of Ayman Al-Zawahiri, Al-Qaida's second-in-command, who asserted, "Terror is from Islam and anyone who denies it is a heretic." The Sheikh relies, among others, on the following Qur'anic surah of the spoils of war:[42]

> *Make ready against them all the power you can [gather], including steeds of war, to strike terror into [the hearts of] the enemies of Allah and your enemies* (Surah 8.60).

The sages of the Shari'a claim that the earlier verses of Mecca which call for peace and tolerance were abrogated (cancelled).[43] The influential Sheikh Yusuf Al-Qaradhawi who appears on Al Jazeera, says that terrorism in Islam is positive and should be welcomed. He draws on Surah 8:12 of the spoils of war: *"I will instill terror into the hearts of the unbelievers: Smite ye above their necks and smite all their fingertips off them."* In a 2003 speech of Eed Al Adha (Festival of the Sacrifice), Usama Bin Laden said, "It is best to follow the blessed terror about which Al-Qaradhawi speaks."

Undoubtedly, the poster child for this brand of Islam is Usama Bin Laden and his Al-Qaida network who are on a Jihad not only against the West, but also anyone in Muslim countries who does not subscribe to their extreme and jihadist version of Islam. The iconic symbol of this Islam is the sword. Tolerance is viewed as a cancer that must be forcefully uprooted. To illustrate, in a speech posted on April 27, 2006, Bin Laden urged Muslims to "kill freethinkers and heretics who defame Islam."[44] Thus, Medinan Islam is violent at its core as it abrogates tolerance and calls for the terror of jihad.[45]

> Medinan Islam is an Islam of terror whose iconic symbol is the sword. Its revelations are believed to cancel the earlier verses of peace and tolerance.

There are two Islams, one with idealistic tendencies, and the other with a sword. Some Muslims view Islam as a religion of peace, while others subscribe to its sadistic call for murder in the name of Allah. However, the promise of heaven, according to the Qur'an, is only for those who heed its call for Jihad. Awaiting those who heed the call are seventy-two virgins to fulfill their every desire. It's no wonder that jihadist Islam has dominated the news. In stark contrast to this dual Islam, Christ is unwavering in His call for love and compassion. Christ does not justify violence under any circumstances, but calls His followers to always love their enemies and pray for those who persecute them.

## Is the Qur'an a Miracle?

The Qur'an challenges those who disbelieve in its miraculous, divine inspiration to produce a surah such as found in the Qur'an. In replying to his good friend Abdallah Ibn Isma'il al

Hashimy concerning this challenge, Al Kindy writes from the court of the caliph Al Ma'moun concerning the Qur'an in ca. AD 830:

> Having been compiled, if not in part composed, by different hands, and thrown unsystematically together, the text is alleged to be in consequence, full of contradictions, incoherencies, and senseless passages. No single argument has been advanced but what is based on evidence accepted by yourselves. And in proof thereof, we have the Qur'an itself, which is a confused heap, with neither system nor order. Now, what could betray greater ignorance than to bring forward such a book as an evidence of Apostleship, and to put it on a par with the miracles of Moses and Jesus! Surely no one with a grain of sense would dream of it; much less should we who are versed in history and philosophy, be moved by such deceptive reasoning.[46]

The German scholar, Salomon Reinach, stated: "From the literary point of view, the Qur'an has little merit. Declamation, repetition, puerility, a lack of logic and coherence strike the unprepared reader at every turn. It is humiliating to the human intellect to think that this mediocre literature has been the subject of innumerable commentaries, and that millions of men are still wasting time in absorbing it."[47]

Moreover, historian Edward Gibbon described the Qur'an as "an incoherent rhapsody of fable, and precept, and declamation, which sometimes crawls in the dust, and sometimes is lost in the clouds."[48]

*McClintock and Strong's Encyclopedia* says:

The matter of the Qur'an is exceedingly incoherent and sententious, the book evidently being without any logical order of thought either as a whole or in its parts. This agrees with the desultory and incidental manner in which it is said to have been delivered."[49]

The German critical theologist and Semitic scholar Ernest Renan points out: "This book (the Qur'an) seems to us declamatory, monotonous, and boring. An uninterrupted reading of it is almost unbearable.[50]

No critical evidence points to the Qur'an as being superior to other Arabic works. In fact, the Islamic scholar, C. G. Pfander, points out: "It is by no means the universal opinion of unprejudiced Arabic scholars that the literary style of the Qur'an is superior to that of all other books in the Arabic language. . . . Some doubt whether in eloquence and poetry it surpasses the Mu'allaqat, or the Magamat or Hariri, though in Muslim lands few people are courageous enough to express such an opinion."[51]

## Imperfections

Muslims contend that the language of the Qur'an surpasses others in composition and eloquence. While Arabs hold their language as the most beautiful in the world, others say their own languages are the most beautiful and hold Arabic as barbarous. If the Arabic language is superior to other languages, then why does the Qur'an contain numerous non-Arabic words? The Qur'an borrows a rich religious vocabulary from Ethiopic and Syriac sources, such as Jewish and Persian religious terms including *Allah, Qur'an, Furqan, Salawat, Jahannam, Janna, Firdaus, Zakat, Deen,* etc. Even the names of biblical personalities are borrowed from Syriac, including Ibrahim, Junus, Musa, Isa, and Idris.[52] But if the Arabic language is superior to other languages, then why would the Qur'an resort to Syriac and Persian to express itself? Is it because the tale of the Arabic Qur'an in heaven was devised to appeal to the Arabs' pride?

Al Kindy asks: "Is it the language that is imperfect while it purported to be the richest and most copious of all tongues, or is it the messenger who lacked command over the language? Better yet, are we to come to abandon the idea that the Qur'an is unchanged, and blame the imperfections on the different people who had a hand in the work over the years?"[53]

> If the Arabic language is superior to other languages, then why would the Qur'an resort to Syriac and Persian to express itself?

Mingana muses, "If we strip away the commentary, the Qur'an is inexplicable." Muslim theologians explain the contradictions by trying to put ayat (verses) in a historical context and by appealing to the doctrine of abrogated and abrogating verses (abrogated verses have been annulled by later abrogating verses).[54]

## Plagiarism

The Qur'an borrows 70 percent of its themes and stories from the Bible. This prompted many scholars to assert that the Qur'an is nothing more than a counterfeit of the Bible. But the Bible is not the only source of the Qur'an, for the Qur'an borrowed four verses and inserted them unchanged from Imraul Qais, one of the most expressive of ancient Arab poets. It was the custom of poets and orators to hang their compositions upon the Ka'aba. When

Qais's daughter heard Fatimah (the prophet's daughter) reciting verses from Qais's poem as though she was reciting from the Qur'an, Qais's daughter demanded to know how her father's verses had become part of a divine revelation (the Qur'an) that is purported to be on eternal stone tablets in heaven.[55] Al Kindy addresses this dilemma ever so eloquently: "I think not that the professors of either [the Taurat and the Bible] would acknowledge thee . . . and would reply that it was simple plagiarism. Nay rather, do thou show us something of thine own, which is in thy hands, and not in ours, but new; and we shall then acknowledge thee to be true and just."[56]

## Scientific Errors

In recent years, Muslims exalted the Qur'an as promoting and supporting science. Critical analysis reveals, however, that the Qur'an is not a scientific marvel as it is self-styled by Muslims. For further insights concerning this, consider its highly controversial claim that human beings come from clots of blood (Surah 23:14). This is hardly a scientific depiction of embryonic development. Other critics note that the Qur'an speaks of Alexander the Great traveling West until he reached the setting place of the sun and found that it sets in a muddy spring (Surah 18:86). This statement has puzzled Muslim commentators over the years who dig themselves in deeper by trying to expound the text in question.[57]

## Grammatical Errors

The Muslim scholar, Ali Dashti, admitted that early Muslims acknowledged that the Qur'an was not a perfect literary piece: "Among the Muslim scholars of the early period, before bigotry and hyperbole prevailed, were some such as Ebrahim An-Nassam who openly acknowledged that the arrangement and syntax of the Qur'an are not miraculous and that works of equal or greater value could be produced."

Dashti expounds on the numerous grammatical irregularities in the Qur'an:

> The Qur'an contains sentences which are incomplete and not fully intelligible without the aid of commentaries; foreign words, unfamiliar Arabic words, and words used with other than the normal meaning; adjectives and verbs inflected without observance of the concord of gender and number; illogical and ungrammatically applied pronouns which sometimes have no referent; and predicates which in rhymed passages are often remote from the subjects.[58]

In summary, over one hundred Qur'anic aberrations from the normal rules and structure of Arabic have been identified.[59]

Furthermore, the Palestinian Islamist scholar, Anis Shorrosh, expounds on the poor grammatical structure of the Qur'an by providing the following examples:

> **The Muslim scholar, Ali Dashti, admitted that early Muslim scholars acknowledged that the Qur'an was not a perfect literary piece.**

- In Surah 2:177, the word *Sabireen* should have been *Sabiroon*;
- In Surah 7:160, the words *Ithnata 'ashrata asbata* should have been *Ithnani 'ashara Sibtan*;

- In Surah 4:143, *walmuquimuna* should have read *wal-muquimina*;
- In Surah 5:69, *al Sabi-eena* should have read *Al Sabi-ouna*;
- In Surah 63:10, *Akun* should have read *Akouna*;
- In Surah 3:59, the words *Kun fa-yakounou* should have read *Kun fakana.*[60]

## Historical Errors

Alphonse Mingana wrote regarding the historical errors in the Qur'an: "Who then will not be astonished to learn that in the Qur'an, Miriam, the sister of Aaron, is confounded with the Virgin Mary? (Surah Al-'Imran 3:35–37) and that Haman is given as minister of Pharaoh, instead of Ahasuerus? (Suratal-Qasas, 28:38). Ignorance of the author of the Qur'an about everything outside of Arabia and some parts of Syria is evident when he makes the fertility and lushness of Egypt—where rain is never missed for the simple reason that it is very seldom seen—depend on rain, instead of on the inundation of the Nile (Surah 12:49). To state, as in Surah Taubah (Surah 9:30), that the Jews believed that Esdras (Ezra) was the son of God, as the Christians thought of the Messiah, is a grave error hardly justifiable. All these historical mistakes are but a shadow of the utter confusion that is made between Gideon and Saul in Surah Baqarah, (Surah 2:250). Such mistakes are indelible stains on the pages of the sacred book which is the object of our study, and they are not wiped out by the following statement: 'We (Allah) relate unto thee a most excellent history, by revealing unto thee this Qur'an, whereas thou wast before one of the negligent' (Surah Yusuf, 12:3)."[61]

## Textual Errors

The Dome of the Rock (ca. 691), the first aesthetic achievement of Islam, presents us with some of the greatest evidence that the Qur'an had been tampered with. Here, one will find inscriptions in blue and gold mosaic decorating the inner and outer faces of the octagonal arcade along with inscriptions on copper plaques on the exterior faces of the lintels over the inner doors of both the eastern and northern entrances. These inscriptions of Qur'anic passages are divergent from the modern Qur'an, particularly the inscriptions on the copper plaques.[62] Here is Islam's third holiest shrine that indicts the inerrancy of the Qur'an and refutes the claim that the Qur'an was not changed.

> The Dome of the Rock, Islam's third holiest shrine, indicts the inerrancy of the Qur'an and refutes the claim that the Qur'an was not changed, as it contains Qur'anic passages that are divergent from the modern Qur'an.

## Pagan Influences

One would be hard-pressed to presume that Islam is the true way to God, because God does not need to borrow rituals, traditions, and holy sites from paganism. Al Kindy writes his Muslim friend who invited him to go on a pilgrimage to Mecca:

> Knowest thou not that the same is practiced of the Sun-worshippers and Brahmas in India at the present day? They make the circuit of their idol temples, with just these ceremonies, shaved . . . or with the dress they call Ihram. . . . Such is the

origin of these idolatrous customs. Thou well knowest that the Arabs practiced them from the foundation of the Ka'aba, and thy master [the prophet Muhammad] continued the same. . . . Thus, that which ye perform in nothing differs from the idolatrous ceremonies of the Sun-worshippers and idolaters of India.[63]

Al Kindy reasons,

Shaving the head, making bare the body, running the prescribed circuits about the Ka'aba, and casting the small stones at Mina, senseless and unmeaning rites, were defended by some as acts of service to the deity; but the worship of God should be conducted, not by unfit and foolish practices, but by observances consonant with reason, pleasing to the Almighty, and edifying to His servants.[64]

## Discrepancies

It is a well-known fact that upon assembling the Qur'an, caliph Uthman had all variant readings of the Qur'an burned, though a few scattered remains are said to have survived. Surah Nur was longer than Surah Bacr, Surah Ahzab had been mutilated, and there was no division between Surah Barat and Surah Anfal. Furthermore, Omar was adamant that the stoning verses were dropped from the Qur'an as well as the ordinance of temporary marriage. In addition, Obey Ibn Kaab mentioned two suras that are no longer extant: Al Kanut and Al Witr. These missing surahs and ayats are the X factor substantiating that many hands changed the revelations to suit their purposes. In summary, Al Kindy pointedly asks: "Are such, now, the conditions of a revelation sent down from heaven?"[65]

## Fallacies

Ali Sina, who left Islam after years of study and investigation, points out the fallacy in the following verse of the Qur'an: *"O you who believe! Take not the Jews and the Christians as awliya' [friends, protectors, helpers, etc.], they are but awliya' [friends] to one another"* (Surah 5:51). Sina reasoned: "I also found the above statement false. The evidence is in the Bosnia and Kosovo crisis, where Christian countries waged war against another Christian country to liberate Muslims. Many Jewish doctors volunteered to help the Kosovar refugees, despite the fact that during WWII, the same Albanian Muslims took sides with Hitler and helped him in his holocaust against the Jews."[66]

## Abrogations

Muslims are adamant in their belief that the Qur'an was written on stone tablets in heaven. But according to the Islamic scholar, William Muir, some two hundred verses have been abrogated or cancelled by later ones that are better. This translates to 3 percent of the Qur'an openly acknowledged as false, although Muslims claim the entire Qur'an is the word of God.[67] Gerhard Nehls remarks concerning this: "We should like to find out how a divine revelation can be improved. We would have expected it to have been perfect and true right from the start."[68] Apparently, Allah of the Qur'an does not share the divine attributes of the God of the Bible but is manlike in his shortcomings. The Bible, however, tells us otherwise: "God is not a man, that he should lie, nor a son of man, that he should change his mind" (Num. 23:19 NIV).

The dilemma of abrogation has necessitated that Muslims develop a whole science around this to explain the rampant Qur'anic contradictions. The greatest challenge of abrogation that confronts Muslims comes from the satanic verses. Mecca's pagans believed that Allah, the moon god, was married to the sun goddess who bore him three goddesses known as the daughters of Allah, who were called Al-Lat, Al-Uzza, and Manat. Although the Meccan pantheon contained 360 gods, Allah and these goddesses were viewed as "high gods" that are superior to all the other pagan deities.[69] In order to placate the Meccans into accepting Islam, while still in Mecca, Islam's prophet allowed for intercession to these pagan idols with the following Qur'anic verses:

> Two hundred verses have been abrogated or cancelled by later ones that are better. This translates to 3 percent of the Qur'an openly acknowledged as false.

> Did you consider Al-Lat and Al-Uzza
> And Al-Manat, the third, the other?
> (Those are the swans exalted);           [later deleted]
> (Their intercession expected);           [later deleted]
> (Their likes are not neglected).[70]      [later deleted]

The Qur'an briefly compromised its' monotheistic message in order to attract more converts. Karen Armstrong, the Islamist scholar, muses that any genuine prophet would have been able to distinguish between holy and satanic revelations. At any rate, the daughters-gate issue remained far more important in the

West until Salman Rushdie wrote his book, *The Satanic Verses* in 1988.[71]

Muslim disciples in Medina rebuked the prophet for falling into polytheism. He later explained that Satan had deceived him, and he thus proceeded to abrogate the last three verses (Surah 53:19–21) that matched the other surahs in style, rhythm, and form. These verses have been deleted (abrogated) from the modern Qur'an. This prompted Meccans to ridicule the prophet, for they asked: "Cannot Allah make up his mind?"[72]

The Muslim scholar Dashti also has asked questions concerning the changeable word of God: "Is it fitting that an All-Powerful, Omniscient, and Omnipotent God should revise His commands so many times? Does He need to issue commands that need revising so often? Why can He not get it right the first time, after all He is all-wise? Why does He not reveal the better verse first?"[73]

Those who deny that the satanic verses were part of the Qur'an need not look farther than the Qur'an which contains references and admission to them: *"And we never sent a messenger or a prophet before thee but when he desired, the devil made a suggestion respecting his desire; but Allah annuls that which the devil casts, then does Allah establish his messages and Allah is knowing, wise"* (Surah 22:52). In addition, the Qur'an blames others for this mishap. *"And surely they had purposed to turn thee away from that which we have revealed to thee, that thou shouldst forge against Us other than that, and then they would have taken thee for a friend"* (Surah 17:73).

The whole concept of abrogation [mansukh] is that divine mistakes are corrected by later verses [naskh]. Besides stripping God of His omniscience, the concept of abrogation also annuls moral absolutes. In other words, truth is not eternal, but relative. It can change depending on the circumstances. Let us examine a simple truth to perceive this absurdity. We hold the fact that God is eternal as absolute truth. Relativism however leaves the possibility open that there might have been a time when God was not eternal. We know that this is a contradiction in terms, because God is either eternal or He is not. If He is eternal, that means it is inconceivable that there was a time when He was not eternal. Thus, if truth can change, then truth becomes extinct.

We must not be surprised that the 124 verses in the Qur'an that encouraged tolerance were now annulled and outmoded by a single verse, called the sword verse, which Bin Laden quoted in his fatwa (religious decree) against the United States: *"But when the forbidden months are past, then fight and slay the pagans wherever ye find them, seize them, beleaguer them, and lie in wait for them in every stratagem [of war]"* (Surah 9:5).

Bin Laden continued in his diatribe: *"And peace be upon our Prophet, Muhammad Bin-'Abdallah, who said 'I have been sent with the sword between my hands to ensure that no one but God is worshipped, God who put my livelihood under the shadow of my spear and who inflicts humiliation and scorn on those who disobey my orders.*[74]

The above command goes against every grain of conscience. Shouldn't religion be about love and overcoming evil with good instead of hatred and bloodshed? No wonder non-Muslims ridicule the idea that Islam is about peace, goodwill, and the brotherhood of men. During the formative years of Islam, Muslim armies slaughtered those who did not accept Islam. Those who were not burned, crucified, or decapitated were heavily taxed [jizya]. Non-Muslims who lived under Muslim rule were treated as second-class subjects. Their women and children were forced to be slaves in order to pay for the crushing Jizya [heavy taxation]. There were two kinds of forced conversions: to choose between Islam or death, or to accept Islam when the burden became too heavy.[75] Even today, Christians are not allowed to repair fallen church walls or paint their churches in Egypt; and Muslims are not allowed to convert to Christianity—those who do are accused of heresy and executed. Why can't people under Islam freely worship without undue burdens?

## The Qur'an Flunks Its Self-Imposed Veracity Test

Irenaeus, the bishop of Lyons and a student of Polycarp, who, in turn, was a student of John the apostle, wrote of the Gospels: "So firm is the ground upon which these Gospels rest, that the very heretics themselves bear witness to them, and, starting from these [documents], each of them endeavors to establish his own particular doctrine."[76] In fact, the Qur'an bears witness to the Bible by adopting 70 percent of its content from the Bible in order to establish its own doctrines. But if we were to strip from the Qur'an the portions drawn from the biblical Scriptures, the Qur'an would implode. Thus, the greatest irony is that the very Scriptures that Muslims claim were corrupted lend a framework to the Qur'an. And even though the Qur'an borrows liberally from biblical narratives, the Qur'an itself is diametrically opposed to the essence of the biblical message. This presents Islam with serious challenges, such as when Allah asked the prophet of Islam in the Qur'an if in doubt of the Qur'anic message to check with the "people of the Book." Hence, according to the Qur'an itself, biblical sources are held in highest esteem and are the yardstick of veracity by which any other message is measured. *"But if thou art in doubt (kunta) as to that which we have revealed to thee, ask those who read the Book before thee. Certainly the Truth has come to thee from thy Lord, so be not thou of the doubters"* (Surah 10:94).

It is clear that the above verse was directed at Islam's prophet, for the verb is in the masculine singular form *kunta* (*you are*), instead of its plural form *kuntum*. However, if we use the biblical source as a yardstick to measure the Qur'anic scriptures, simply put, the Qur'an flunks the acid test of veracity because it rejects the fundamental tenets of Christianity—the Trinity, the inerrancy of the biblical Scriptures, the deity of Christ, His death on the cross, and His resurrection.

In comparing the Qur'an and the Bible concerning inerrancy, consider the following:

- The Qur'an contradicts the Bible concerning fundamental issues. They cannot both be right; one of them must be in error.
- The Qur'an claims that the Bible is the barometer of truth.
- Therefore, the Qur'an must be in error.

1. **The Qur'an contradicts the Bible concerning fundamental issues.** They cannot both be right: one must be in error:
   a. Regarding the identity of Jesus, the Qur'an says, *"They indeed disbelieve who say: 'Surely, Allah — He is the Messiah'"* (Surah 5:17, see also 5:72).
   b. Regarding the crucifixion of Jesus, the Qur'an says, *"They killed him [Jesus] not, nor did they cause his death on the cross, but he was made to appear to them as such"* (Surah 4:157).
2. **The Qur'an claims that the Bible is the barometer of truth.**

a.  *"But if you are in doubt as to what We have revealed to you, ask those who read the Book [Bible] before you"* (Surah 10:94a).

b.  *"And that which We have revealed to you of the Book [Bible], that is the truth verifying that which is before it; most surely with respect to His servants Allah is Aware, Seeing"* (Surah 35:31).

c.  *"Say: Who revealed the Book which Moses brought, a light and a guidance to men?"* (Surah 6:91b).

d.  *"And do not dispute with the followers of the Book except by what is best, except those of them who act unjustly, and say: We believe in that which has been revealed to us and revealed to you, and our God and your God is One, and to Him do we submit"* (Surah 29:46).

3. *Therefore, the Qur'an must be in error.* Since the Qur'an and the Bible disagree on fundamental issues, they cannot both be right. Logic demands that one has to be in error. Muslims claim that since the Bible does not match the Qur'an, the Bible must have been corrupted. However, since the Qur'an teaches that the Bible is the barometer of truth, this leads to the inevitable conclusion that whenever the Bible and the Qur'an disagree, the Qur'an must be in error. In other words, the Qur'an is in error concerning a myriad of theological issues such as the Holy Trinity, the identity of Jesus as the Son of God, the sacrificial atonement of Christ, and the inerrancy of the Bible. Let us examine some clues in the following vignette to explain why the Qur'an is so vastly different from the Bible.

"A cartoon shows a line of pews and the same verbal sentence is being passed from one pew to the other:

| First pew: | "My ear kind of hurts." |
| Second pew: | "The pastor has an earache." |
| Third pew: | "The pastor got a hearing aid." |
| Fourth pew: | "The pastor is having trouble hearing." |
| Fifth pew: | "The pastor got a double earring." |
| Last pew: | An old lady with a cane is walking out out and says, "That does it, I'm outta here! The pastor's got a double earring!"[77] |

Though it is intended to be satirical, the above vignette brilliantly describes how biblical stories could be altered in the Qur'an. The main reason behind the discrepancies between the Bible and the Qur'an is that Islam's prophet had to rely on oral information from Christians and Jews concerning the Bible. At this time in history, the Bible had not yet been translated into the prophet's language of Arabic. It was eventually translated into Arabic approximately three hundred years after his death. This further proves that the Qur'an lacks divine origins, for biblical stories would have been preserved unchanged. Muslims need to make up their minds concerning whether Allah's word can be altered. If it cannot be altered, then the Bible, which the Qur'an claims to be the Word of God, could not have been altered. Muslims cannot vacillate on their beliefs concerning this issue to suit their purposes while still claiming intellectual honesty.

Let's employ the same technique used above to evaluate the inerrancy of the Bible by letting the Qur'an speak for itself on the issue:

- The Qur'an claims that the Bible is the Word of God.
- The Qur'an claims that God's Word is inerrant.
- Therefore, the Bible must be inerrant.

1. *The Qur'an claims that the Bible is the Word of God:*
   *And believe (O children of Israel) in what I have revealed, veri-*
   *fying that which is with you, and be not the first to deny it, nei-*
   *ther take a mean price in exchange for My communications; and*
   *Me, Me alone should you fear* (Surah 2:41).

   *Say: We believe in Allah and [in] that which had been revealed*
   *to us, and [in] that which was revealed to Ibrahim [Abraham]*
   *and Ismail [Ishmael] and Ishaq [Isaac] and Yaqoub [Jacob] and*
   *the tribes [12 tribes of Israel] and [in] that which was given to*
   *Musa [Moses] and Isa [Jesus], and [in] that which was given to*
   *the prophets [biblical prophets] from their Lord; we do not make*
   *any distinction between any of them, and to Him do we submit*
   (Surah 2:136).

   *Say: O People of the Book, you follow no good 'til you observe*
   *the Torah and the Gospels and that which is revealed to you from*
   *your Lord. And surely that which has been revealed to thee from*
   *thy Lord will make many of them increase in inordinacy and dis-*
   *belief; so grieve not for the disbelieving people* (Surah 5:68).

See also Surahs 2:285; 3:3, 48, 70, 184; 5:44, 46, 77; 6:91, 154;
11:110; 17:2, 4, 14; 19:12, 30; 21:7; 23:49; 25:35; 28:2, 43, 52; 29:46;
32:23; 37:117; 40:53; 41:45; 45:16; 57:25, 26, 27a; 62:5; 98:4.

2. *The Qur'an claims that God's Word is inerrant:* And certainly
   *apostles before you were rejected [biblical prophets], but they were*
   *patient on being rejected and persecuted until Our help came to*

*them; and there is none to change the words of Allah [meaning that the Bible could not be altered], and certainly there has come to you some information about the messengers (Surah 6:34).*

*He said: The knowledge thereof is with my Lord in a book [the Bible]; my Lord neither errs nor forgets (Surah 20:52).*

*(Such has been) the course of Allah that has run before, and thou wilt not find a change in Allah's course (Surah 48:23).*

See also Surahs 10:34, 37; 56:78.

3. ***Therefore, the Bible must be inerrant.*** If the Bible is inerrant, Muslims must believe the Bible. We have already established that the Bible is God's Word and that Muslims must believe all of God's revelations in order to be saved. Since God's Word is inerrant, Jesus Christ has to be the Son of God who was crucified and raised from the dead to atone for the sin of humankind. Furthermore, there's no salvation except through Him. Any Muslim who disagrees with this conclusion undermines the integrity and infallibility of their own scriptures. Their own Qur'an convicts them:

*But the unjust deny the communications of Allah (Surah 6:33).*

*Surely they who disbelieve in the communications of Allah, they shall have a severe chastisement; and Allah is Mighty, the Lord of retribution (Surah 3:4).*

Muslims must remember that the Qur'an considers Jesus a prophet and issues a strong warning to those who reject God's prophets:

*Seest thou not those who dispute concerning the messages of
Allah? How are they turned away? Those who reject the Book and
that with which We have sent Our Messengers. But they shall soon
know. When the fetters are on their necks and the chains. They are
dragged into hot water; then in the Fire they are burned* (Surah
40:69–72).

In summary, if Muslims believe their own scriptures, they
must believe what the Bible says concerning Jesus—that He is the
Son of God who manifested the grace of God to fallen humanity.

## Conclusion

Over the centuries the orthodox Muslim community, out of reverence for their holy book, have been reluctant to take a rational
and critical approach to the Qur'an and its origins. Those who dare
to do so are confronted with a barrage of evidence to dispel any
consideration that the Qur'an was divinely inspired. One encounters confusion, contradiction, and disorientation upon evaluating
the Muslim holy book. The Islamist author Patricia Crone states
in her works that "the Qur'an is a text without a context."[78] This
is readily apparent when the Qur'an introduces biblical terms such
as the Holy Spirit or the Messiah without any amplification concerning their meanings. Consequently, without commentary from
Islamic scholars, who do not always agree on interpretation, the
Qur'an is baffling and mysterious. But should God's Word be
incommunicable? Is God not a God of order, who is capable of
revealing His Word without human assistance?

In the Bible, God confirmed the messages of his prophets
with signs and wonders so people would believe. When John the
Baptist was imprisoned, he sent his disciples to ask Jesus, " 'Are you

the expected One, or shall we look for someone else?' Jesus
answered and said to them, 'Go and report to John what you hear
and see: the blind receive sight and the lame walk, the lepers are
cleansed and the deaf hear, the dead are raised up, and the poor
have the gospel preached to them. And blessed is he who does not
take offense at Me" (Matt. 11:3–6).

Jesus produced even greater signs and wonders than these, for
He rose from the dead and later "appeared to more than five hundred brethren at one time" (1 Cor. 15:6). The Qur'an, however,
offers no evidence of its divine authorship to searching hearts. The
whole of the Qur'an is built on the testimony of one man without signs, wonders, or prophecies. Islam's prophet was the only
person to experience the giving of Islamic revelations [tanzil] in
direct contrast to the Bible. Meanwhile, the Jews physically expe-
rienced the presence of God in a cloud by day and a pillar of fire
by night and observed countless miracles, such as the ten plagues
of Egypt and the splitting of the Red Sea. They literally saw God
in action during the dramatic showdown between Elijah and the
prophets of Baal (see 1 Kings 18:20–40). Therefore, the fact that
Islamic tanzil is inconsistent with Biblical revelations casts doubts
on whether Islam hails the same God, since God's nature is
unchanging.

How can rational, intelligent minds believe the Qur'an when
it states that there can be no change in the words of God (Surah
10:64), especially since the Qur'anic revelations are riddled with
contradictions? God is eternally holy. Neither God nor His Word
changes. His teachings in the Bible can be summarized like this:
"You shall love the Lord your God . . . , and you shall love your
neighbor like yourself" (Matt. 22:36, 37, 39).

It's impossible to find such a call for unconditional love in
Surah 9:5 of the Qur'an where one finds an open war cry for

bloodshed. Since the Qur'an was enforced at the point of the sword without miracles or proofs, and since it is riddled with imperfections, confusion, and discrepancies, it follows that the whole of Islam falls to the ground. The Christian's understanding of the holiness of God leaves no room for imperfections. As a result, one must reject the claims that the Qur'an is divinely inspired by the God of the Bible.

> After reviewing the overwhelming evidence concerning the variability of the Qur'an, one must reject the claims that the Qur'an is divinely inspired by the God of the Bible.

# Was the Prophet Muhammad a Biblical Prophet?

*The one who does not love his brother whom he has seen, can-not love God whom he has not seen. And this commandment we have from Him, that the one who loves God should love his brother also (1 John 4:20, 21).*

## Critical Analysis of the Prophet Muhammad

Evidence is the means by which disputed facts are proven true or false in any court of law. Likewise, evidence is the tool of choice in the trade of critical analysis as it discounts preconceived notions, biases, and emotions and helps to establish material facts.

Many questions abound concerning Islam's prophet, Muhammad. People on both sides of the aisle mechanically draw on their viewpoints, whether of emotions or facts. But where does the evidence point concerning Islam's prophet who counts 22 percent of the world's population among his followers? This chapter will raise and address the following questions to help unveil the mystery of one of the most influential men in the history of the world.

- Was Islam's prophet, in the tradition of biblical prophets, an instrument of the Almighty chosen to point humanity to the right path, or was he concerned with the things of this world?
- Did a display of miracles punctuate his ministry to confirm him as the Almighty's chosen one?
- Was he an implement of justice, a force of righteousness who protected the rights of the powerless?
- Was he a man of peace sent to usher in a new age of harmony, reconciliation, and compassion?
- Did the so-called messenger of Allah further the brotherhood of people, or did he sow seeds of hatred?
- Was he merciful to his enemies, or did he leave a trail of blood and terror behind him?
- Did the so-called prophet foretell the future accurately in the pattern of true biblical prophets?
- Did the hand of the Almighty protect him from harm and endow him with triumph whenever a challenge arose?
- Were the fruits of his ministry peace and harmony, or were they war and bloodshed?
- Did he advance an earthly kingdom marked with military power and plunder, or did he set his sights on the afterlife?

Let's examine these questions in the ensuing sections.

## Heavenly Pursuits or Earthly Trappings?

Was the prophet Muhammad a biblical prophet or an earthly king? According to Henri Lammens, the Orientalist scholar, "The obstinate politics of Muhammad and his struggles against the Jews had made him the biggest real estate owner of the Hijaz (Arabia). He possessed vast domains in Medina, Khaybar, Fadak, and Wadi Qora."[1] Muhammad's view of religion was vastly different from that of Jesus, who did not have a place to lay his head. Islam's prophet amassed earthly riches and affluence. Once Muhammad became powerful, he no longer was satisfied with modestly crouching on a leather cushion or leaning against a palm tree while presiding during Friday meetings in the Masjid (Arabic for Mosque). But in the ways of the Abyssinian and Syrian imperial governors, he sat on a throne placed on a platform. Eventually, he had a whole collection of pulpits, some more exotic than others, which he used according to the occasion.[2]

> Muhammad's view of religion was vastly different from that of Jesus, because Islam's prophet amassed earthly riches and affluence.

Lammens insightfully describes the ostentatious royal display of Islam's prophet:

> From this height, from what was both a throne and a platform, he would lecture the crowds, not standing up as the old-fashioned tradition claimed, but sitting in the fullness of his authority as a legislator and of his prestige as a King-Prophet. In his hand he held a sort of scepter ['asa, qadib]; a stick [mihjan] made of precious wood, encrusted with gold and ivory; and a short spear or javelin ['anaza] like the command batons artistically fashioned that the Byzantine government gave to the barbarian chieftains who rallied to the Empire. If he had to move, his attendants carried this insignia in front of him, when it pleased him to hand it to them. Once installed in his pulpit, he took it back and used

it to emphasize parts of his speech. Also in the imitation of imperial governors, he had chamberlains and heralds known as mo'addin or monadi. On important days, Bilal [mo'addin] would precede the prophet, unfolding a sort of canopy above his head. When Muhammad presided in the minbar, Bilal would stand at the foot of the throne, an unsheathed sword in his hand.[3]

Although the prophet Muhammad cautioned his followers to abstain from worldly luxuries in order to enjoy them in the next world, he did not himself abstain from flamboyant display and luxury. He dazzled the Bedouins with his wardrobe that included a large red cloak [chlamys], silk tunics, crimson robes, and a beautiful coat richly trimmed in gold. He allowed members of his inner circle [sahabis] to wear silk; even he himself distributed rich silk tunics, one of which he gave to the austere Ibn Al Khattab who hastened to sell his so as not to sacrifice the silk tunics reserved in paradise. The prophet Muhammad also had a spacious scarlet leather tent—a symbol of grandeur and power—that he set up in the courtyard of the mosque for the reception of deputations. In the prophet's majlis (seat) were Persian hangings, damask materials from Syria, and carpets from the East. There was a glittering scene of scarlet and gold on the heavy door curtains. As a result, "the good example for his followers" paraded flamboyant displays of wealth and power fit for a king, while counseling his followers to lead lives of modesty and humility. Even after the hardship of the hijra (emigration to Medina), the prophet Muhammad and his immediate circle did not adopt the austere conception of life set forth in the principles of monasticism.[4]

Thus, the prophet's ostentatious pursuit of power and wealth presents us with a clear example of the maxim, "Don't do as I do, but do as I say." Consequently, Islam's prophet comes across as an earthly king seduced by the riches of this world instead of an ascetic biblical prophet who set his sight on the Creator and the afterlife.

> Islam's prophet comes across as an earthly king seduced by the riches of this world instead of an ascetic biblical prophet who set his sight on the Creator and the afterlife.

## Women

The prophet Muhammad used to state that his chief passions were women, wealth, food, and scents. Lammens points out the temptations of the prophet: "the passion for women, the desire for male children, the thirst for gold, silver, and spirited horses, and the possession of cattle and land, in fact all the pleasures of such like on earth."[5] This explains why, despite the Qur'an's directive for Muslims not to exceed four wives, the prophet allowed himself fifteen wives (records vary on exact number of wives) and two handmaidens after a self-serving revelation. The prophet's relationships with women also reveal his feet of clay. He was not above fury, anger, and rage; in fact, by his own admission, he was one of us, a mere mortal. The prophet's daughter, Fatima, who was married to Ali, was anemic; but when the prophet caught her resting during the day, he would kick her brutally. Furthermore, if he met her on the streets of Medina, he would rudely challenge her: "What has pushed you out of your house?"[6] These customs helped shape Islam. Furthermore, they help explain why to this day, women in Saudi, the seat of Islam, have subservient roles and are denied the most basic rights, such as driving. The prophet also made chauvinistic comments such as, "Hell is filled with women." This does not paint a rosy picture concerning women in the eyes of the prophet. It casts them as trophies, instead of human beings who are created in the image of God.

## Character

The earliest biography of the prophet Muhammad was written by the Muslim, Ibn Ishaq, who died in AD 768 (130 years after the prophet's death). Although the actual manuscripts perished, their contents survived in the form of quotations by later authors such as Ibn Hisham (in Sirat An Nabbi) and Al Tabari. Fortunately, the work of Ibn Ishaq reflects freethinking, as it did not come under the influence of later idealizing tendencies. This work paints a picture of Islam's prophet based on two primary sources, the Qur'an and tradition [Ahadith].

Arthur Jeffery summarizes the biography of the prophet Muhammad by Ibn Ishaq as follows:

> The character attributed to Muhammad in the biography of Ibn Ishaq is exceedingly unfavorable. In order to gain his ends he recoils from no expedient, and he approves of similar unscrupulousness on the part of his adherents, when exercised in his interest. He profits to the utmost from the chivalry of the Meccans, but rarely requites it with the like. He organizes assassinations and wholesale massacres. His career as tyrant of Medina is that of a robber chief, whose political economy consists in securing and dividing plunder, the distribution of the latter being at times carried out on principles which fail to satisfy his followers' ideas of justice.

He [the prophet Muhammad] is himself an unbridled lib-
ertine and encourages the same passion in his followers. For
whatever he does, he is prepared to plead the express autho-
rization of the deity. It is, however, impossible to find any
doctrine that he is not prepared to abandon in order to secure
a political end. At different points in his career he abandons
the unity of God and his claim to the title of prophet. This is
a disagreeable picture for the founder of a religion, and it
cannot be pleaded that it is a picture drawn by an enemy.

Though Ibn Ishaq's name was for some reason held in
low esteem by the classical traditionalists of the third Islamic
century, they made no attempt to discredit those portions of
the biography which bear hardest on the character of their
prophet.[7]

If Islam's prophet was truly sent as a mercy aid to humankind,
why then, according to his own admission, were women, wealth,
scents, and food his chief delights in life? Are these earthly lusts
and desires fitting for a prophet of the Almighty? Why would he
attack peaceful tribes or trade caravans? Was it not to pillage, plunder, and kill so he could carry off new wives, concubines, and
earthly treasures? Are those expressions of mercy?

Furthermore, in what is known as the prophet's worst scan-
dal, he swore that he would not go near his wives for a whole
month, but having lost his patience, he approached them before
the appointed time.[8] Would a biblical prophet break his oath?

Al Kindy, who worked in the court of the caliph Al Ma'mun,
points out in his famous apology to his Muslim friend Abdallah
Ibn Ismail the Hashimite (cousin of the caliph), how the prophet
lost his first three expeditions, thus missing his plunder and retir-
ing crestfallen:

Judge now for yourself whether Muhammad could have been a prophet, as thou sayest. And what concern have prophets with plunder and pillage? Why did he not leave raids and forays to brigands and highwaymen? Tell me wherein the difference lies between thy Master (Muhammad) and Babek Khurramy,[9] whose insurrection hath caused such grief . . . and disaster to mankind at large? I know well thou canst not answer this. And so it continued all through thy Master's life, even until he died. If a caravan was weak, he attacked it, plundering and slaughtering; but if strong, he fell back and fled.[10]

While deliberating Muhammad's character, we should evaluate Allah's view of his prophet. Upon mentioning the name of the prophet of Islam, Muslims speak the words "Sallah 'llah 'alaihee wa sallam." Muslims accept the words of *pbuh* ("peace be upon him") as an acceptable translation. However, these words in my native language of Arabic are literally translated: "God, pray upon him and salute him with peace." The original text actually implies that God prays for the prophet. If indeed God did pray, to whom would He pray? Isn't God all-powerful and all-sufficient? Isn't He the Creator of all and the uncreated one? Isn't He from everlasting to everlasting? This perplexing *pbuh* statement flies even in the face of Muslim theology concerning Allah's character.

## Assassinations

Muslims refer to their prophet as a "blessing and mercy to mankind." It's worthwhile noting, however, that in addition to the prophet leading sixty-six wars against his enemies, according to historians, he ordered a series of assassinations against his enemies, the first of which was of an elderly Jew. In the biography of the prophet entitled *Sirat Rasul Allah,* Ibn Ishaq, the Muslim historian of Islam's second century (hijra dating), details several such incidents. According to Ibn Ishaq, the prophet asked his followers: "Who will rid me of Ibnu'l Ashraf?" One of the prophet's followers offered to kill him for the prophet, but said that in order to kill him, he must lie to him first. The prophet replied that it was okay to lie so long as the enemy was eliminated. The obedient follower then proceeded with his evil deed, and Muhammad praised him for it.[11]

Another incident concerns the daughter of Imra'ul Quais who was later put to death. Her crime—she had dared to point out that the prophet Muhammad plagiarized one of her father's poems that was hanging from the Ka'aba and included it as a Qur'anic revelation.

The prophet's deepest disappointment in his career was the Jewish rejection of his prophethood. The Jews knew the Scriptures and could not reconcile the glaring inconsistencies between the Qur'an and their own Scriptures. In retaliation, the prophet Muhammad issued a command to his followers: "Kill any Jew that falls into your power." Ibn Ishaq relates a story about when the prophet and his followers took over a town after they learned that a treasure was hidden there. The prophet threatened a man who knew the whereabouts of the treasure: "We will kill you if you don't tell us," but since the man refused to reveal the location of the treasure:

> The apostle Muhammad gave orders to al-Zubayr, "Torture him until you extract what he has." So he kindled a fire with a flint and steel on his chest until he was nearly dead. Then the apostle delivered him to Muhammad b. Maslamah and he struck off his head.[12]

The actions of the prophet Muhammad, as conveyed by a Muslim historian and biographer (supported by the Ahadith) are not consistent with the actions of biblical prophets. Jesus told the disciples of John the Baptist to tell John that the miraculous events, such as how the blind were receiving sight, the lepers were being cleansed, the deaf were hearing, and the dead were being raised up came from his direct connection with the Father (see Luke 7:22). Unfortunately, the guiding principles of the prophet Muhammad and his followers could not have been even remotely associated with a loving and merciful God. Moreover, the actions of Islam's prophet could certainly not be reconciled with the command that Jesus laid down, which is to love our neighbors like ourselves (see Matt. 22:39).

> The actions of Islam's prophet could certainly not be reconciled with the command that Jesus laid down, which is to love our neighbors like ourselves.

Islam's prophet presents humanity with situational ethics that are not about right and wrong or good and evil. Islam's code of ethics does not transcend circumstances or mirror the holiness of God. Instead, truth becomes a variable where the end justifies the means, even if it entails abrogating the Word of God and breaking the Ten Commandments in the process.

Shouldn't the fruits of a prophet of the Almighty be mercy, benevolence, and brotherhood instead of cold-blooded murder? How can anyone with integrity justify lying and defend the killing of a helpless old man (Ibnu'l Ashraf) simply because he did not accept Islam? Is it right to exterminate a people (the Jews), enslave their women and children, and impound their possessions simply because they rejected Muhammad as a prophet sent by the Almighty? Isn't it morally reprehensible to have the daughter of Imra'ul Quais killed because she dared point to the plagiarism of one of her father's poems in the Qur'an? Is it intellectually honest to cloak assassinations under the guise of "surrendering to God" (Islam means surrender)?

> **Shouldn't the fruits of a prophet of the Almighty be mercy, benevolence, and brotherhood instead of cold-blooded murder?**

Cold-blooded murder is evil. Love is superior to hatred. Freedom is more precious than suppression. Truth is more noble than plagiarism.

## Miracles?

In stark contrast to Jesus Christ, the prophet of Islam did not have a single supernatural sign witnessed by multitudes and referenced in the Qur'an like the miraculous feats of Jesus. The prophet Muhammad never raised the dead. He never healed the blind or the paralytic. He was not resurrected from the dead, nor did he ascend into heaven in front of others. Although the prophet Muhammad claimed that he was taken up to heaven during the night of power, there were no witnesses, no one to verify these claims. There was no one to touch and feel these wonders like doubting Thomas did when he felt the nail marks in Jesus' hands. When asked to show signs and miracles, the prophet Muhammad replied that he was only a man (Surah 17:93). Jesus on the other hand, performed miracles that only God can do and claimed unity with God, "He who has seen Me has seen the Father" (John 14:9).

When the prophet was attempting to proselytize the Qurayshites, they said,

> Well, Muhammad, since you . . . persist in pretending to be the messenger of God, give us clear proofs of your prophethood. Our valley is narrow and sterile, get God to widen it, get Him to move apart these mountain chains, which confine it, from one another; let Him make rivers flow like those in Syria or Iraq, or better still let Him make some of our ancestors rise from their tombs, . . . and let these illustrious resurrected dead acknowledge you as prophet, then we will also recognize you as such.

The prophet replied that God did not send him for this sort of thing but only to preach His law.[13] How convenient it was for the prophet Muhammad to accomplish the most amazing feats when he had no witnesses, such as his alleged travel to the sacred rock in Jerusalem and subsequent ascent through the seventh heaven. However, he was unable to perform the smallest miracle in the presence of witnesses.

The Qurayshites said to the prophet Muhammad, "At least, ask your Lord to make appear one of His angels as a witness to your truthfulness and to order us to believe you." Once again, the prophet refused their pleas. They then asked him, "Well, let your Lord make the sky fall on us, as you maintain that He is able to do, for we shall not believe you."[14] It seems that the prophet, who, according to his own testimony, frequented the company of angels, should be able to persuade them to be visible to others, at least for a brief moment!

Even the Qur'an records such encounters when Muhammad's critics demanded miracles of him to prove that he was in the tradition of biblical prophets:

*And they say: We will by no means believe in you until you cause a fountain to gush forth from the earth for us. Or you should have a garden of palms and grapes in the midst of which you should cause rivers to flow forth, gushing out. Or you should cause the heaven to come down upon us in pieces as you think, or bring Allah and the angels face to face (with us) (Surah 17:90–92).*[15]

The answer of the prophet, however, was unequivocal. It was that he was a mere mortal apostle. The Semitic scholar Ernest Renan said of Islam's prophet: "We can follow . . . his contradictions, his weaknesses. . . . Muhammad, Omar, and ʿAli are neither seers, visionaries, nor miracle workers. . . . Each one reveals himself naked and with all the weaknesses of humanity."[16] Thus, the question of the lack of miracles is not one that Muslims can easily shake off while maintaining that Muhammad is the greatest of Biblical prophets.

In the famous Christian vs. Muslim debate between Anis Shorrosh and Ahmed Deedat in 1985 at the Prince Albert Hall in London, England, the articulate Muslim scholar Deedat attempted to dismiss the validity of the book of Revelation in the Bible by claiming that it was a dream.[17] Deedat's choice of words was rather interesting. In what is known as the night of power, Islam's prophet claimed to have taken a nocturnal journey to Jerusalem on the back of a human-faced donkey-mule by the name of Burak, and from there, he purportedly went through the seven heavens to see the biblical prophets and the Almighty. Things, however, turned out badly for the prophet Muhammad as his followers greeted this story with a storm of derision. In fact, many followers retracted their allegiance. Faced with ridicule, the prophet Muhammad retracted the idea that this transcendental fantasy was real by saying that it was only a dream.[18] Interestingly, this was the same choice of words of the late Mr. Deedat—it was only a dream.

## Hand of the Almighty

Muhammad nearly lost his life during the battle of Uhud when a tooth was broken, his lip was split open, his cheek and temple were dashed, and his face was covered with blood by a sword at the hands of Otba. Talha, the prophet's companion, saved the prophet's life by shielding him from Otba's sword, but Talha lost his fingers in the process.[19] There could not have been a more opportune time for Islam's prophet to produce miracles than during this incident. He could have restored Talha's fingers and healed his own wounds if he had the power to do so in the same way that Jesus restored the ear of the high priest's servant in the Garden of Gethsemane before He was crucified (see Luke 22:50, 51). It is painfully clear that Islam's prophet did not have the power to perform healing. If we don't see the finger of God in Islam, then how can we be certain that God is the author of Islam?

Muslims state that Allah does not allow his prophets to suffer. Maulana Muhammad Ali, the Muslim theologian and prolific author of several classic works on Islam (titled section 6 of Surah 21) in his translation of the Qur'an states: "Allah always delivers Prophets."

Following are some instances, however, when Allah did not deliver the prophet Muhammad:

- He was pelted with stones upon proselytizing Zeyd.
- His face was struck with a sword during the battle of Uhud, which he lost when the Qurayshites were cut to pieces as he was fighting alongside them against the Hawazin.[20]

- He fell off his horse, was thrown against a palm tree, and sprained his foot.
- He bit into the shoulder of the poisoned goat that Zainab had prepared for him and suffered agonizing pain and later died as a result of the poisonous effects.[21]

If "Allah always delivers his Prophets" as Muslims claim, then where was Allah when Islam's prophet needed deliverance? Where was the angel Gabriel who is regarded as the protector of the prophet (Surah 66:4)?

Muslims cast aspersions on Muhammad's career as a prophet when they hold on to the belief that God could not have allowed Jesus to suffer on a cross.

It's clear that if Islam's prophet were a biblical prophet sent by the Almighty, then surely, the hand of the Almighty would have been visibly with him. The German critical theologian and Semitic scholar Ernest Renan reasons:

> It must seem surprising that one sent by God could suffer defeat, see his prophecies thwarted, and win half-victories. In the great supernatural legends, things are very differently managed; there, all is clear-cut, absolute as it should be when God interferes . . . He [Muhammad] is defeated, he makes mistakes, he retreats, he corrects himself, he contradicts himself. Muslims acknowledge up to two hundred and twenty-five contradictions in the Qur'an, that is to say two hundred and twenty-five passages which were later abrogated, within the perspective of another policy. One cannot deny that on several occasions, Muhammad consciously did harm knowing perfectly well that he was obeying his own will and not an inspiration from God. He allowed brigandage,

he ordered assassinations, and he lied and permitted lying as a stratagem of war. One could cite a host of circumstances where he compromised morality for political ends. One of the most peculiar instances of that is assuredly when he promised 'Uthman forgiveness in advance for all the sins that he might commit until his death, in return for a large financial sacrifice.[22]

Isn't God sovereign? Doesn't His moral perfection emanate moral absolutes, infinite justice, and truth? But if these things which are the characteristics of the Almighty are absent, how can one intelligently claim that the hand of the Almighty sanctioned and blessed Islam's prophet?

## Prophecies

Biblical tradition found in Deuteronomy 18:20–22 provides us with an acid test of whether a prophet speaks in the name of the Lord. A true prophet unfolds the future with pinpointed accuracy. The prophet Daniel, for instance, predicted the exact date of the Messiah's entry into Jerusalem, which happened exactly 483 years later (see 9:25–27). However, the fact that the vision of the prophet Muhammad only extended to the past, casts serious shadows on his career as a prophet.

A single verifiable prophecy appears in the Qur'an and gets a nod from Islamic scholars. It's the prophecy of Al Rum (the Romans) where Islam's prophet predicted the triumph of Muslim armies over the Romans in ten years (Surah 30:1–4). This lone prophecy, however, is riddled with problems, as both the demise of the Roman Empire and the rising power of Islamic armies was equally self-evident. Therefore, it did not take a prophet to predict the eventual defeat of the Romans. The issue, however, is that it took the armies of the prophet twelve years from the acceptable date of the prophecy to subdue their enemies instead of ten. According to the word, *Bid' 'i*, which is used to describe when the victory would take place, the victory should have occurred between no less than three years and no more than nine years. Therefore, the prophet Muhammad missed the deadline of his prophecy by three years.[23]

In addition to the self-evident prophecy that the then teetering Romans would be defeated, some scholars point to a predictive prophecy that Muhammad revealed. It was a self-fulfilling prophecy that he would return to Mecca. However, in stark contrast to this prophecy, Jesus predicted that He would return from the grave (see John 16:22).

If the acid test of a prophet is to predict the future with pinpointed accuracy, then the absence of predictive prophecy in the Qur'an refutes the claims of Islam's prophet that he was a prophet in the biblical tradition. Muhammad flunks the prophets' test by lacking prophetic utterances that are the basic ingredient of biblical prophets. Many historical sources, including Byzantine literature, represented Islam's prophet as an epileptic, which explains his "revelatory trances." In addition, Spanish Christians were deeply troubled by the prophet's sexual immorality.[24] Consequently, once we stack up the life, character, and example of Islam's prophet, he fails to measure up to the predefined pattern of the biblical prophets.

## Justice?

One would presume that the prophet Muhammad was a guardian of the oppressed and a defender of justice. In order to evaluate this assumption, turn your attention to one Hadith story, which by all accounts is stranger than fiction.

> A thief was brought to the prophet (peace be upon him). He said: "Kill him." The people said: "He has committed theft, Apostle of Allah!" Then he said: "Cut off his hand." So his (right) hand was cut off. He was brought a second time and he (the prophet) said: "Kill him." The people said: "He has committed theft, Apostle of Allah!" Then he said: "Cut off his foot." So his (left) foot was cut off. He was brought a third time and he (the prophet) said: "Kill him." The people said: "He has committed theft, Apostle of Allah!" So he said: "Cut off his hand." So his (left) hand was cut off. He was brought a fourth time and he (the prophet) said: "Kill him." The people said: "He has committed theft, Apostle of Allah!" So he said: "Cut off his foot." So his (right) foot was cut off. He was brought a fifth time and he (the prophet) said: "Kill him." So we took him away and killed him. We then dragged him and cast him into a well and threw stones over him.[25]

That instance was a flagrant contradiction of the following Qur'anic admonition revealed when Aisha (the prophet's favorite wife) was accused of infidelity. The prophet's defense of his beloved Aisha conveniently came in the form of a revelation, and stated that the accusers needed to produce four witnesses: *"Why did they not bring four witnesses to prove it? So, as they have not brought witnesses, they are liars in the sight of Allah"* (Surah 24:13).

Ironically, however, when it came to the thief, the prophet threw due process out the window. He condemned the man in a lawless, vigilante fashion without witnesses or a trial hearing.

Furthermore, the punishment did not fit the crime. The prophet
Muhammad decreed in other instances that a reasonable punishment for theft is that the hand of the thief be cut off. In one case,
he ordered the hand cut off and hung on the neck of the thief.[26]
Thus, once again, one is left with the overwhelming sense that
Islam has no moral absolutes, for justice or truth change depending on the situation. Note the theatrics of these judgments as well
as the clear lack of humility. Every time the thief was brought to
the prophet, it seems as if he wanted to outdo the previous command as if to impress his audience by his moral superiority. One,
however, cannot help but feel a great sense of injustice. By contrast, ponder the words of Jesus: "Why do you look at the speck
that is in your brother's eye, but do not notice the log that is in
your own eye?" (Matt. 7:3). Muhammad purportedly prayed seventy times a day for Allah to forgive his sins, but his attitude in this
situation depicts an overwhelming sense of pride instead of humility in light of his own sins.

If Allah of the Qur'an is called Al Rahman Al Raheem (the
Compassionate, the Merciful), why is his prophet so far removed
from mercy and compassion? Is Allah hard of hearing since the
prophet Muhammad prayed seventy times a day to forgive his sin?
Did Allah not have the power to forgive sin, or did the prophet
Muhammad keep on sinning? Would a biblical prophet slaughter
his enemies simply because they did not believe him to be a
prophet? Was the one who built an earthly kingdom with the
sword the messenger of a loving God? Is the one who prayed
incessantly for God to forgive his own sins, be in a position to tell
us how to have our own sins forgiven? Would a prophet of God
hear from the devil and believe it was from God (in the case of the
satanic verses which were later rescinded)? Would a prophet of
God question his own sanity to the point of wanting to commit

suicide? Could a prophet speak for the Creator when he presented the Creator as a vacillating entity who could not make up his mind, thus issuing contradicting revelations at every turn?

One can only conclude that Islam's prophet, Muhammad, had feet of clay and was a sinner just like all humanity.

## The Death of the Prophet Muhammad

The most potent words of people are those they utter on their deathbeds. This is the moment of truth when people are transparent before their Maker, when they drop their masks, and the finality of life unveils blatant realities. People cut through the fog and articulate the essence of their fears. So what were the last words the prophet of Islam whispered on his deathbed on June 8, AD 632? "Lord, grant me pardon; eternity in Paradise! Pardon. The blessed companionship on high."[27]

The prophet with the sword, who waged war in sixty-six recorded battles, asked for forgiveness for his sins because he was insecure about his own salvation.

The religion of Islam never promises the assurance of salvation or absolute forgiveness (except for murdering jihadists). Instead, people's good deeds are weighed in the scales of justice against their evil deeds on the Day of Judgment. If the good deeds weigh more than the evil deeds and if Allah wills it, then they enter paradise. In other words, Muslims may spend their entire lives following the pillars of Islam without having the assurance of everlasting life—for in Islam, only Allah knows. This is in sharp contrast to Christianity that offers the assurance of salvation, not according to our works, for they will never measure up to God's standards, but according to God's grace manifested in Jesus Christ.

In his expository book, *Muhammad et la Fin du Monde* (*Muhammad and the End of the World*), Casanova reveals that Islam's prophet believed he lived in prophetic times. He believed that "the times announced by Daniel and Jesus had arrived: Muhammad was the last prophet chosen by God to preside conjointly with the Messiah who was to return to earth for this purpose, at the end of the world and the final judgment." The prophet Muhammad firmly believed he would witness the final dissolution of the world before he died. When he felt death overtaking him, he was in dreadful distress since his prophetic insight was proven wrong. Upon his death, his immediate followers refused to believe the news of his passing. Casanova reasons that some of the curious phenomena in the Qur'an is due to its being re-edited to square with the fact of Muhammad's death.[28]

Once he knew that death was upon him, the prophet Muhammad believed he would rise from the dead after three days because he was too honorable for God to leave him on earth. In fact, after he died, his followers cried: "How can he be dead? Did we not count upon him to be our witness on the Day of Resurrection? He is not dead! He hath been carried up to Heaven, even as was Isa (Jesus). Beware, lest ye bury him!"[29]

When the anticipated resurrection never took place, his followers were forced to bury him on the fourth day due to the progress of decay in his body. As a result, most of his followers became disillusioned and apostatized, but were eventually brought back by the Abu Bakr—some by persuasion, others by intimidation, fear, and the sword, and still others by the prospects of wealth and power.[30] Thus, unlike that of Jesus, the earthly death of the prophet Muhammad was definitive. Muhammad's death sent shock waves to his closest followers who were dismayed by the sudden finality of his ministry without a single observable supernatural event they could point to as indisputable evidence that the Creator had sent him and that He was indeed with him.

## Why Is Prophethood Only for the "Children of Israel"?

When Adam disobeyed God in the garden (Surah 2:36; 20:115, 121), he broke his fellowship with God (Surah 7:22a; 20:121a) and was expelled from the garden as a result (Surah 2:36–38). Since Adam is depicted in the Qur'an as representing humankind (Surah 2:34; 7:11; 38:72), it follows that Adam sinned on behalf of all. This truth is self-evident because humankind was subsequently banned from the garden. But what happened after Adam was expelled from the garden?

To answer the above question, follow the clues the Qur'an provides that are found in Surah Al Baqarah. This surah (chapter), the largest in the Qur'an, is organized into three parts, forty sections, and 286 verses. It deals mainly with the Jews. Its fourth section covers the greatness of humans over the angels (Surah 2:34; see 2:30–39) and how Iblis (Satan) made Adam and Eve sin in the garden and depart from the state they were in (Surah 2:36). After the fall of Adam, the surah switches immediately to section 5 concerning the Israelites (Surah 2:40–46). There, the Qur'an reminds its readers of the favor God bestowed on the people of Israel. It admonishes them to be faithful to their covenant with God and promises that God will fulfill His covenant with them. Section 6 concerns the divine favor on Israel. God reminds Israel how He made them excel among the nations (Surah 2:47). But that raises the following questions:

1. How does Israel relate to the fall of Adam and removal from the garden?

2. Why did God favor the Israelites?
3. What is the nature of the covenant God made with Israel?

The Qur'an answers the above questions as follows:

1. *Israel is God's only prophetic voice:* "*And certainly We gave the Children of Israel the Book and judgment and prophethood and provided them with good things, and made them excel in the nations*" (Surah 45:16).

2. *God set them apart to reveal Himself to the world through them.* Israel was to preserve the God-inspired Scriptures and to share God's love and mercy with the rest of the world. The Qur'an is also explicit that God chose the Jewish people for a pre-designed plan: "*And We granted him Is-haq [Isaac] and Yaqoub [Jacob], and caused the prophethood and the Book to remain in his seed, and We gave him his reward in this world, and in the hereafter he will most surely be among the good*" (Surah 29:27).

3. *In His covenant with Abraham, Isaac, and Jacob, God promised to send the Messiah through their descendants for the salvation of humankind.* Jesus was the fulfillment of God's prophetic promises that God would send a Savior to the world. Jesus came from the line of Abraham, Isaac, and Jacob through a virgin woman as God promised. God's judgment for the sins of all people fell on Him. The spiritual death that humans suffered in the garden can now be overcome by the blood of Jesus. God's promises came true, so why would He send another prophet with a contradictory message, preaching salvation by works instead of grace? Even the Qur'an asserts that the Jews have the

prophethood. Thus, the idea that Islam offered a different path to God is troubling to say the least.

## Are There Biblical Prophesies Concerning Muhammad?

Jesus said of His ministry: "If I alone testify about Myself, My testimony is not true. There is another who testifies of Me" (John 5:31–32). Some Muslims point to Deuteronomy 18:18 as speaking of the prophet Muhammad: "I will raise up a prophet from among their countrymen like you, and I will put My words in his mouth, and he shall speak to them all that I command him." This verse, however, finds its fulfillment in John 4:25, 26, when Jesus witnessed to the Samaritan woman who referred to this prophecy: "The woman said to Him, 'I know that Messiah is coming (He who is called Christ); when that One comes, He will declare all things to us.' Jesus said to her, 'I who speak to you am He.'"

The prophet Muhammad never claimed to be the long-awaited Messiah, who was to come for the salvation of the Jews and Gentiles, but he reserved that title for Jesus. For that reason, Muhammad ruled himself out as the possible fulfillment of that prophecy. Moreover, the prophet Muhammad did not even have a forerunner to prepare the hearts of the people for a Messiah, like John the Baptist. The coming of Islam's prophet wasn't anticipated, nor did signs and miracles accompany him. He simply claimed to be a messenger of God without any evidential miracles. Even if one were to ignore the overwhelming evidence that Deuteronomy 18:18 finds its fulfillment in the Messiah, then why aren't there hundreds of prophecies foretelling the coming of Islam's prophet in the Bible? As mentioned earlier, Muslims answer that question by claiming that the Bible was corrupted, but should a critic make such claims without an iota of evidence, especially when the Bible is supported by countless archeological discoveries that prove that it has remained unchanged over the years?

## A Symphony of Contrasts

Islam and Christianity are the two largest faiths in the world, but their respective main prophets could not be further apart. In concluding this section, it is worthwhile to summarize some of those differences:

1.  There were no prophecies predicting Muhammad's coming, while Jesus fulfilled countless prophecies.
2.  Muhammad had a natural birth, while Jesus was supernaturally born of a virgin.
3.  Some of Muhammad's revelations were self-serving, such as making it legal to marry his daughter-in-law, while Jesus' revelations were self-sacrificing, such as being crucified for the sins of the world.
4.  Muhammad performed no miracles, while Jesus healed lepers, gave sight to the blind, walked on water, and raised people from the dead.
5.  Muhammad established an earthly empire, while Jesus said His kingdom was not of this world.[31]
6.  Muhammad admitted that his chief passions were women, scents, and food, while Jesus' chief passion was to glorify the name of His heavenly Father.[32]
7.  Muhammad was an earthly king who amassed wealth, becoming the richest landowner in Arabia, while Jesus did not have anywhere to lay His head.[33]

8. Muhammad was marked by the sword, while Jesus was marked by love.

9. Muhammad encouraged Jihad, while Jesus said that "those who take up the sword shall perish by the sword."[34]

10. If a caravan was weak, Muhammad attacked it, plundering and slaughtering; if it was strong, he fled. In contrast, Jesus said, "Let your light shine before men in such a way that they may see your good works, and glorify your Father who is in heaven."[35]

11. Muhammad had an adulteress stoned,[36] while Jesus forgave an adulteress.[37]

12. Muhammad married fourteen women, including a seven-year-old girl, while Jesus had no sexual relations.

13. Muhammad recognized he was a sinner, while Jesus was sinless even by Qur'anic accounts.[38]

14. Muhammad did not predict his death, while Jesus predicted the exact time of His crucifixion and subsequent resurrection.[39]

15. Muhammad did not nominate or train a successor, while Jesus prepared His successors.

16. Muhammad was so insecure concerning his salvation that he prayed for forgiveness seventy times a day, while Jesus was the essence of salvation, for He said: "I am the way, and the truth, and the life; no one comes to the Father but through Me."[40]

17. Muhammad slaughtered his enemies, while Jesus died for His enemies.

18. Muhammad died and remains buried, while Jesus rose from the dead.[41]

# Is Allah the God of the Bible?

*How great is the love the Father has lavished on us, that we should be called children of God! . . . Dear friends, let us love one another, for love comes from God. Everyone who loves has been born of God and knows God. Whoever does not love does not know God, because God is love. This is how God showed his love among us: He sent his one and only Son into the world that we might live through him. This is love: not that we loved God, but that he loved us and sent his Son as an atoning sacrifice for our sins . . . (1 John 3:1; 4:7–10 NIV)*

## The Origins of Allah

During the days of Noah, God destroyed the earth with a flood because its inhabitants except Noah and his family, increased in wickedness and worshiped pagan deities. After the Flood, Arphaxad, Noah's grandson through Shem, settled in Ur of the Chaldees (located in the region of Babylon in modern-day Iraq). It was déjà vu, for despite God's judgment of sin during the days of Noah, iniquity increased greatly in the earth, as people, including Abram and his family, became wicked and idolatrous (see Josh. 24:2). God wanted pagan worship to be a thing of the past. He wanted to set a people apart from polytheism unto Himself as a God-centered moral nation so He could reveal Himself to the world through them.

God chose Terah's (Abram's father) line for this task. He asked him to leave his idolatrous people and religion behind and move to Canaan. Terah left Ur, the sophisticated Chaldean metropolis, with his son Abram, his daughter-in-law Sarai, and his nephew Lot, but he never made it to Canaan. Instead, he became complacent and settled in Haran (modern-day Syria) where he eventually died.[1] Abram however, heeded God's call. He left Haran and its idolatry and went to Canaan. God planned to show humankind the path to Himself through Abram's seed (descendant), resulting in God changing Abram's name to Abraham—"the father of many nations" (see Gen. 17:1–5). But it was many years before Abraham and Sarah had a child. When Abraham was ninety-nine years old, God told him that his ninety-year-old wife, Sarah, would bear a child—the child of promise through whom the Messiah would come for the salvation of the world.

Ur of the Chaldees and Haran were the chief centers of worship of Sin during the time of Abraham (ca. 2100 BC). Sin was the moon god of Semitic religions and a principal deity in the Babylonian and Assyrian pantheons. Given the sheer number of artifacts concerning the moon god discovered throughout the Middle East, archeologists concluded that this cult was the most popular religion all through ancient Mesopotamia.

The Assyrians, Babylonians, and Akkadians transformed the Semitic word *Suen* into the word *Sin* as their favorite name for this deity.[2] Sin however had many names in the

> God wanted to set a people apart from polytheism unto Himself as a God-centered moral nation so He could reveal Himself to the world through them.

Ur of the Chaldees from which God called Abraham, was so devoted to the moon-god that it was sometimes called Nannar (after Nanna— moon god) in tablets from that time period. Sir Leonard Woolley excavated a Babylonian temple of the moon god from that time period. His discoveries are displayed in the British Museum. Note the presence of the crescent moon (on the left).[6]

Likewise, during the time of Abraham, the important city of Haran

had the moon deity as patron god, under the name of Sin. To the right are Sin's star and crescent as found on a coin in Haran.[7]

A major temple of the moon god was excavated in the 1950s at Hazor in Palestine. The inscription confirmed that the two idols found were in fact statues of the moon god. Each statue was of a man sitting on a throne, with a crescent moon carved upon his chest.[8]

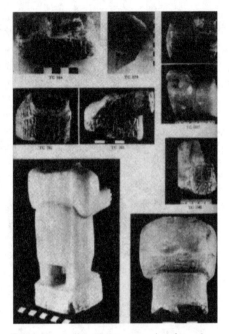

The adjacent worship tablet shows arms outstretched toward the moon god here represented by the full moon within the crescent moon.[9]

Several smaller idols were also found in Hazor. These were identified by their inscriptions as the daughters of the moon god (known in Mecca prior to Islam as Al-Lat, Manat, and Al-Uzza).[10]

region but was primarily known as Nanna,[3] Hubal,[4] and later Allah.[5]

Thus, archeological evidence reveals that the moon god, whose symbol throughout Arabia was the crescent moon—the iconic symbol of Islam—was worshiped by the people of Mesopotamia, especially Ur, Haran, Sumeria, Assyria, Babylon, Syria, Canna, Persia, and Egypt. Southern Arabia was steeped in the worship of the moon god, as substantiated by the thousands

In Persia (top right), as well as in Egypt (center), the moon god who is depicted on wall murals and on the heads of statues was considered the judge of men and gods. The bottom right depicts the similarity between the pre-Islamic and Islamic crescent-and-star glyphs. Anatolian (center), Islamic (right).[11]

of Sabean, Minaean, and Qatabanian inscriptions of the moon god dug up in the nineteenth century and subsequently translated by Arnaud, Halevy, and Glaser.

Archeologists G. Caton Thompson and Carleton S. Coon confirmed their work in the 1940s. Wendell Phillips, W. F. Albright, Richard Brower, and others who excavated Qataban, Timna, and Marib, capital of Sheba, made further archelogical discoveries in southern Arabia concerning the moon god in the 1950s. All the excavated statues, wall murals, seal impressions, steles (pillars), pottery, amulets, clay tablets, cylinders, weights, earrings, necklaces, etc. of the moon god sported a crescent moon. Furthermore, temples of the moon god were also excavated in Ur, Hazor, and Hureidha, where statues were also found of the daughters of Allah—the moon god—known in Arabia as Al-Lat, Al-Uzza, and Manat.[12]

## The Moon God and Israel

Two generations after Abraham moved to Canaan, in the days of Jacob (Abraham's grandson), the Israelites (descendants of Abraham through Jacob whose name God changed to Israel) went to Egypt because of a famine in Canaan. Four hundred years later, after Moses led the Israelites back to the Promised Land, the land inhabitants primarily worshiped the moon god.[13] The Israelites never completely cleansed the land from the idolators. This disobedience was to cost them dearly. Even though God blessed Abraham and made his descendants into a great nation, the ghost of the pagan moon god of the Canaanites haunted the Israelites. Soon, the Israelites began worshiping the moon god of the Canaanites.[14] (See Deut. 4:19; 17:3; 2 Kings 21:3–5; 23:5; Jer. 8:2; 19:13; Zeph. 1:5.)

## Allah in Islam

It would be brutally dishonest to claim that Muslims do not have the sovereign creator in mind when they think of Allah. Islam is clearly against moon worship, *"Adore not the sun and the moon, but adore Allah who created them."* (Surah 41:37)

Islam teaches monotheism in the unequivocal terms. It's a grave sin of *shirk* [polytheism] to associate anything or anyone with Allah. For this reason, the Muslim creed of faith begins with "La Illaha Illa Allah" (There is no god but God).

The French writer and philosopher Ernest Renan said, "Religions are facts; they must be discussed as facts, and subjected to the rules of historical criticism."[15] With this thought and using the rules of historical criticism, I will examine the inception of Allah into Islam. In doing so, I will draw liberally on direct quotes to safeguard the original intents of the authors.

## The Misuse of the Name "Allah"

The word Allah is used to denote the creator in Arabic Bibles. In fact, Arab Christians called God "Allah" long before Muhammad appeared on the scene.

The word "Allah" simply means "the god" and corresponds to "ho theos" in the Greek New Testament as "the God" which refers to the Father in John 1:1 and the Son in John 20:28 and Heb 1:8. What is interesting is that Hubal was the top pagan moon god of the Kabah. So Allah is the generic and Hubal, may have been the actual name, in the same way that "the God" is generic and "Jehovah" is the name. The Arabs may have referred to "Hubal" as "Allah", just like Jews would refer to "Jehovah" as "The God."[16]

> "Allah, the Islamic word for God . . . was originally applied to the Moon."

The scholar John Van Ess elaborates on pagan adaptations of Allah.

At Mecca, Allah was the chief of the gods and the special deity of the Quraysh, the prophet's tribe. Allah had three daughters: Al Uzzah (Venus) most revered of all and pleased with human sacrifice; Manat, the goddess of destiny, and Al Lat, the goddess of vegetable life.[17]

Another scholar states, "Allah, the Islamic word for God . . . was originally applied to the Moon."[18] Furthermore, Ibn Warraq, the ex-Muslim and great student of Islam contends that Allah was eventually applied to the supreme deity in Mecca.[19]

## The Moon God Hubal

Martin Ling, a scholar of Islam, describes the origin of Hubal, "A chieftain of theirs (Khuza'ah tribe), on his way back from a journey to Syria, had asked the Moabites to give him one of their idols. They gave him Hubal, which he brought back to the Sanctuary, setting it up within the Ka'bah itself; and it became the chief idol of Mecca."[20]  In his book, *Muhammad, the Holy Prophet*, Hafiz Ghulam Sarwar reveals that the Meccans placed Hubal on the roof of the Ka'aba, suggesting that Hubal was the chief deity (Allah) of the Meccans.[21] Wellhausen, a leading German scholar of the nineteenth century points out that when the Meccans defeated Muhammad in a battle, their leader shouted: "Hurrah for Hubal." This led to the conclusion that "Hubal is none other than Allah, the "god" of the Meccans."[22] In his book, *Muhammad the Holy Prophet*, Hafiz Ghulam Sarwar states, "Besides idol-worship, they also worshiped the stars, the sun and the moon." [23]

The world religion scholar Peter Occhiogrosso paints the religious backdrop of Mecca.

Before Muhammad appeared, the Kaaba was surrounded by 360 idols, and every Arab house had its god. Arabs also believed in jinn (subtle beings), and some vague divinity with many offspring. Among the major deities of the pre-Islamic era

> Hubal, the chief idol of the Meccans, was a Moabite god known as the moon god.

were al-Lat ("the Goddess"), worshiped in the shape of a square stone; al-Uzzah ("the Mighty"), a goddess identified with the morning star and worshiped as a thigh-bone-shaped slab of granite between al-Taif and Mecca; Manat, the goddess of destiny, worshiped as a black stone on the road between Mecca and Medina; and *the moon god Hubal, whose worship was connected with the black stone of the kaaba. The stones were said to have fallen from the sun, moon, stars, and planets and to represent cosmic forces. The so-called black stone* [actually, the color of burnt umber] *that Muslims revere today is the same one that their forebears* [ancestors] *had worshiped well before Muhammad and that they believed had come from the moon.*[24] (author's emphasis)

The black stone that Occhiogrosso refers to is a meteorite that is still venerated by Muslims to this very day. It sits in a corner of the Ka'aba, the Muslim holy shrine, and continues to be kissed by Muslim pilgrims. Maximus Tyrius, who lived during the second century, wrote of the Ka'aba and its' black stone, "The Arabians pay homage to I know not what god, which they represent by a quadrangular stone."[25] The black stone was placed next to Hubal, which strongly suggests that Hubal was connected with moon worship.

George W. Braswell, Jr, another Islamic scholar, confirms the account of Occhiogrosso concerning the Ka'aba. Braswell states,

Pre-Islamic Arabia also had its stone deities. They were stone statues of shapeless volcanic or meteoric stones found in the deserts and believed to have been sent by astral deities. The most prominent deities were Hubal, the male god of the Ka'ba, and the three sister goddesses al-Lat, al-Manat, and al-Uzza; Muhammad's tribe, the Quraysh, thought these three goddesses to be the daughters of Allah. Hubal was the chief god of the Ka'ba among 360 other deities. He was a man-like statue whose body was made of red precious stone and whose arms were of solid gold.[26]

According to Khairt al-Saeh, who studied Arab myths and legends, "Hubal was associated with the Semitic god Baal and with Adonis or Tammuz, the gods of spring, fertility, agriculture, and plenty."[27] When the Israelites fell into idolatry, they worshiped the Canaanite god, Baal, and his consort Asherath, represented by Venus. Asherath, also known as Ashtarout, was known and worshiped in Mecca as Al-Uzza. Al-Uzza was considered one of daughters of Allah. She, along with her sisters Al-Lat and Manat, were the subject of the *The Satanic Verses* made famous by Salman Rushdie.

Sam Chamoun who studied the sources of Islam states, "Interesting is the name $H_UB_AL$ (in Arabic and Hebrew script the vowels were not noted). This shows a very suspicious connection to the Hebrew $H_AB_{AA}L$ (= the Baal), an idol mentioned in the Bible (Num. 25:3, Hosea 9:10, Deut. 4:3, Josh. 22:17 and Ps. 106:28, 29)."[28] Thus, we might infer that Hubal (or Baal) is the god the Israelites worshiped whenever they fell into idolatry.

## The Transformation From Hubal to Allah

In his book, *A History of Arab Peoples*, Albert Hourani writes, "The name used for God was 'Allah,' which was already in use for one of the local gods." [29] Scholar S.M. Zwemer writes, "But history establishes beyond the shadow of a doubt that even the pagan Arabs, before Mohammed's time, knew their chief god by the name of Allah and even, in a sense, proclaimed his unity . . . Among the pagan Arabs this term denoted the chief god of their pantheon, the Kaaba, with its three hundred and sixty idols."[30] Since the notion of a chief god was pervasive in Mecca prior to Islam, Ibn Warraq states, "Islam owes the term "Allah" to the heathen Arabs." [31]

In *Muhammad's Mecca*, W. Montgomery Watt states, "There are stories in the Sira of pagan Meccan praying to Allah while standing beside the image of Hubal".[32] This suggests that they were at one time praying to Allah through Hubal, or said differently, Hubal was their Allah. However, one must observe that the two eventually became distinct. Karen Armstrong, the scholar on world religions states,

The Ka'aba was dedicated to al-Ilah, the High God of the pagan Arabs, despite the presiding effigy of Hubal. By the beginning of the seventh century, al-Ilah had become more important than before in the religious life of many of the Arabs. Many primitive religions develop a belief in a High God, who is sometimes called the Sky God. . . . But they also carried on worshipping the other gods, who remained deeply important to them.[33]

Scholar Carl Brockelmann states,

The more the significance of the cult declined, the greater became the value of a general religious temper associated with Allah. Among the Meccans he was already coming to take the place of the old moon-god Hubal as the lord of the Ka'bah. . . . Allah was actually the guardian of contracts, though at first these were still settled at a special ritual locality and so subordinate to the supervision of an idol. In particular he was regarded as the guardian of the alien guest, though consideration for him still lagged behind duty to one's kinsmen.[34]

Karen Armstrong provides added insight to this transformation at the Ka'aba, "Officially, the shrine (Ka'aba) was dedicated to Hubal, a Nabatean deity . . . but by Muhammad's day, it seems that the Ka'aba was venerated as the shrine of Allah, the High God (monotheistic deity).[35]

Kenneth Cragg, the scholar on Islam, sheds further light on the dynamics of the Meccan transformation from polytheism to monotheism, "The Prophet's mission was not to proclaim God's existence but to deny the existence of all lesser deities."[36]

The polytheists in Mecca already recognized Allah as the creator before the advent of Muhammad. Yet it's rather naïve to believe as Muslims do, that Allah who was worshiped by the pagans did not have an idol in the Ka'aba. The evidence suggests that Hubal was the original representation of Allah to Meccans. By the time of Muhammad however, Meccans who were longing for a form of monotheism of their own similar to the Jews and Christians, began to gradually divorce Allah from Hubal. This however, was a perverted form of monotheism for Meccans refused to abandon the worship of their pagan deities, but they wanted their Allah to co-exist with paganism.

When Islam's prophet entered Mecca victorious, he had all 360 pagan deities in the Ka'aba destroyed. Thus, he was making a clear break from the idolatrous ways of the polytheists and embracing pure monotheism under the name of Allah. Karen Armstrong writes, "Muhammad did not think that he was founding a new religion but that he was merely bringing the old faith in the One God to the Arabs, who had never had a prophet before."[37] The scholar of Islam, Nodelke adds, "In any case it is an extremely important fact that Islam's prophet did

> Hubal was originally the representation of Allah in the Meccan mind. However, Meccans began to transform Allah into an independent deity.

not find it necessary to introduce an altogether novel deity, but contented himself with ridding the heathen Allah of his companions subjecting him to a kind of dogmatic purification."[38]

## The Fusing of Allah and Paganism

It is troubling however, that Islam retained pagan customs and practices and fused those with the worship of Allah. "Islam took over—or rather, retained—the following customs from the pagan Arabs: polygamy, slavery, easy divorce, and social laws generally, circumcision, and ceremonial cleanliness. Wensinck, Nodelke, and Goldziher have all contributed to the study of the animistic elements in the rituals connected with Muslim prayer"[39] Dr Robert Morey who studied Islam also states that Islam adopted the pagan rites, rituals, and ceremonies associated with this cult which remain a part of Islam to this day. "These include, praying toward Mecca several times a day; making a pilgrimage to Mecca; running around the temple of the moon god called the Ka'aba; kissing the black stone; killing an animal in sacrifice to the moon god; throwing stones at the devil; fasting for the month that begins and ends with the crescent moon; giving alms to the poor; and so on."[40]

> Islam retained pagan customs and practices and fused those with the worship of Allah.

Phillip Hitti, author of the *History of the Arabs,* explains that the Bedouin astral belief centered on the moon, since Bedouins grazed their flocks in its light. Hitti explains that moon worship implies a pastoral society and that "Bedouins imagine that their life is regulated by the moon, which condenses the water vapors, distils the beneficent dew on the pasture, and makes possible the growth of plants. On the other hand the sun, as they believe, would like to destroy the Bedouins as well as all animal and plant life."[41] By adopting the iconic crescent of the moon god, Islam forever cemented the worship of Allah with the idolatrous moon god.

Moreover, the cult of the Sabeans that is mentioned favorably in the Qur'an, admitted to the existence of astral spirits and the worship of stars. According to the scholar Al Sharastani, some Sabeans worshiped the stars directly while others worshiped man-made idols that represented the stars in temples similar to the Ka'aba. The influence of the Sabeans in the Qur'an is not a secret, as per the prevalence of oaths by the stars and planets:

*"I swear by the falling of the stars"* (Surah 56:75).

Furthemore, Surah 53 is entitled "The Star" and begins with, *"By the star when it plunges."* Also, Surah 54 is entitled "The Moon"[42] and Surah 91 is entitled "The Sun." Meccans had 360 idols in Mecca, one for every day of the lunar year. Muir suggests that Muslims encircle the Ka'aba seven times to symbolize the motions of the seven planets.[43] Interestingly, the Sabaeans even had a moon god whose specific appellation was "Allah"[44]

Although the daughters of Allah were all venerated in the Meccan pantheon, Jack Finegan points out in his great work, *The Archeology of World Religions*, that the Aus and Khazraj tribes of Medina worshiped Manat more prominently, but that Muhammad's

> Although Islam used the name Allah, it also incorporated pagan customs and rituals into Islam. All of this indicates that the conception of Allah in Islam does not denote the eternal God of the Bible.

tribe, the Quraysh of Mecca, paid much reverence to Al-lat (also represented by the crescent moon) and Al Uzza. Finegan continues: "As the moon and the evening star are associated in the heavens, so too were Al-Lat and Al-Uzza together in religious belief, and so too are the crescent and star cojoined on the flags of Arab countries today"[45] (see exhibits A and B). For these reasons, although Islam used the name Allah, it also incorporated pagan customs and rituals into Islam. All of this indicates that the conception of Allah in Islam does not denote the eternal God of the Bible.

## Summary

One scholar of Islam, Caesar E. Farah, stated: "Allah, the paramount deity of pagan Arabia, was the target worship in varying degrees of intensity from the southernmost tip of Arabia to the Mediterranean . . . With Muhammad, he (Allah) becomes Allah, God of the worlds."[47] Wellhausen also cited pre-Islamic literature that alludes to Allah as a great deity.

Although Arabs continued to worship other deities, the worship of the moon god (Allah) became pagan Arabia's answer to the monotheistic Judeo-Christian faith around them. Soon the polytheists of Arabia recognized Allah as their own monotheistic deity. They swore by him (Surah 6:109) and recognized him as the Creator (Surahs 23:84–89; 29:61) well before the advent of Muhammad. This may explain why the literal translation of the Islamic creed Allahu Akbar is "Allah is greater" instead of "Allah is great" implying that Allah is greater than the other gods.

Pagans in the Arabian Peninsula felt they had been left out of the divine plan. As a result, they longed for a prophet of their own who spoke to them in their own language. They believed that their old religions had failed them given that their society was

Exhibit A: The moon god idol, found in Palestine dating back to AD 0 to 600. It depicts the crescent moon (Al Lat)–feminine form of Allah and which is also represented by the moon- cojoined with the morning star (Al Uzza).[46]

Exhibit B: Muslim flags depicting the symbols of the moon god.

1st column: Afghanistan, Algeria, Azerbaijan, Brunei, Comoros, and Emirate of Umm al-Qaiwan,

2nd column: Malaysia, Malaysian City of Kuala Lumpur, Malaysian state of Johor, Malaysian state of Kedah, Malaysian state of Kelantan, and Malaysian state of Malacca,

3rd column: Malaysian state of Selangor, Malaysian state of Terengganu, Maldives, Pakistan, Red Crescent (similar to Red Cross), and Singapore,

4th column: Tunisia, Turkey, Turkish Republic of Northern Cyprus, Uzbekistan, and Western Sahara.

bursting with social ills and falling apart at the seams. They were exposed to the idea of monotheism from their Jewish and Christian neighbors, so they longed for a monotheism of their own. The Judeo-Christian monotheism, however, was not good enough for them because their version of monotheism had to be on their own terms. It had to preserve what was dear to them such as their pagan Ka'aba, its' black stone, and its associated hajj (pilgrimage which brought them revenues). It had to allow them to continue their old pagan practices of polygamy, easy divorce, throwing stones at the devil, running between two hills that had idols on them, etc. For them to accept monotheism, it had to meet their own agendas and satisfy their own requirements. Theirs had to be a custom monotheism with their unmistakable stamp. To illustrate the absurdity of these pagan customs, Caliph Omar said while addressing the black stone at the Ka'aba, "Had I not seen the Prophet kiss you, I would not kiss you myself"[48]

Though the name Allah denotes the eternal God of the Bible, the concept of Allah in Islam is steeped in pagan rituals. Islamic leaders did not produce anything new but kept some of the old and borrowed just enough good from monotheism to suit their purposes. What they kept, however, was not a full measure of God. They took offense at the blood of the Lamb on the cross of Calvary—the ultimate manifestation of God's divine love. In so doing, they swept humankinds' sin and rebellion under the rug. Islam presented a god of the sword instead of a God of the cross, a god who avenges instead of a God who loves, and a distant, impersonal god, instead of a God of close relationships who longs for intimate communion with his creation.

As a result, Islam does not have a god of mercy and grace, but a vengeful and bloodthirsty god of the moon. The moon god Hubal, the antithesis of the God of the Bible, was the original representation of Allah in the Meccan mind. Slowly they transformed Allah into an independent deity. Had they been sincere in following the true God, they would have followed Him as He revealed Himself in the Bible. This led Zwemer to conclude, along with a myriad of Islamic scholars, that Islam "is not an invention, but a concoction; there is nothing novel about it except the genius of Muhammad in mixing old ingredients into a new panacea for human ills and forcing it down by means of the sword."[49]

By fusing the moon god with monotheism, Islam's prophet must have envisioned that this unholy marriage between the sacred and the profane, idolatry and monotheism, could placate both the polytheists and the followers of the one true God of Abraham. In the beginning during the Meccan religious modifications, the original Qur'anic revelations were flattering to Jews and Christians. However, since the Jews of Arabia did not embrace the worship of Allah, they were systematically stripped of their wealth, slaughtered, enslaved, or banished from the land.

Then when Islam's prophet called for a return to the true religion of Abraham, he must have been referring to Abraham's religion prior to his conversion—which was none other than the worship of the moon god. The Hanifite faith was, in fact, the idolatrous faith of the Sabeans who worshiped the starry hosts and are affectionately referred to in the Qur'an. This is the religion Abraham professed before his call and subsequent conversion to worshiping the one true God.[50]

The conclusion is that the worship of Allah of the crescent is nothing short of polytheism with a face-lift. What good is it that Islam called its followers to monotheism if that monotheistic deity came with a long list of pagan credentials?

Today, the Jihadists embark on bloodshed, while believing that Allah will reward their evil deeds with seventy virgins each in paradise. Even the most basic understanding of the character of the God of the Bible reveals that He is love; but if Allah is God, then why would he be the author of such hatred? How could a loving God who is the essence of holiness, goodness, and purity sanction such malevolence?

The data conclusively shows that despite the fact that the god of Islam shares the same name as the God of the Bible, the god worshiped by Muslims is not the same God of the Bible. Islam clearly has a fixation with the moon god. Why else is the crescent moon the symbol of Islam and adorns the flags of many Muslim countries? Why else would it dominate the top of mosques and minarets everywhere? Why else would the timing of the *hilal* [the crescent moon] mark the starting the Ramadan, the Muslim holy month of fasting? Why else would Muslims partake in animism under the guise of monotheism by kissing the stone (black stone) of the moon god? Why else would Muslims preserve pagan customs and practices such as circumambulating a pagan temple? Why else would their god demand of his adherents the shedding of blood?

Caesar Farrah puts it best in his analysis concerning the notion of Allah in Islam, "There is no reason, therefore, to accept the idea that Allah passed to the Muslims from the Christians and Jews."[51]

## Allah the "Abrogator"

The Hijra was a defining moment in Islam. It occurred when, due to the persecution of Muslims, the prophet Muhammad joined his followers in an emigration from his ancestral homeland, Mecca, to the welcoming Medina. There, Muhammad found himself for the first time in a position of power that allowed him to return to monotheism, which was his original call. He proceeded to abrogate the earlier Qur'anic revelation that allowed the worship of Allah's three daughters—Al-Lat, Al-Uzza, and Manat (shirk or polytheism)—whose worship he had sanctioned while in Mecca in order to appease the Meccans.

As a result of the preceding event, one is left with unanswered questions. Should the Quraish (the prophet's tribe) have accepted Muhammad's revelations? And should the Hijra never have occurred? In other words, had the Quraish accepted Islam, and had the Hijrah never occurred, would Muslims still be worshiping the daughters of Allah today?

The most troubling aspect concerning Allah of the Qur'an is that he changes his word at will. His word does not seem to stand the test of time. The end result is that the Qur'an is full of contradictory verses. As such, the militant Islam of Medina subsumed the peaceful Islam of Mecca. The Qur'an attempts to explain the concept of abrogation (cancellation) in the following surah: *"Whatever communications We abrogate or cause to be forgotten, We bring one better than it or like it. Do you not know that Allah has power over all things?"* (Surah 2:106).

Abrogation however casts Allah in a troubling light. The concept of abrogation leads one to the following conclusions concerning his character in the Qur'an, despite Muslim assertions to the contrary:

- Allah must not be omniscient. He makes mistakes like the rest of us. Allah cannot discern the future; otherwise, he would have provided the better revelations in the first place.
- Allah must not be omnipotent. Muslims acknowledge that the Bible is the Word of God, but since the Bible does not match the Qur'an, they claim that the Bible was corrupted. If Allah is omnipotent, then why could he not

> **Allah is manlike in his shortcomings as evident by erroneous revelations that he later corrects.**

protect his word from corruption? Furthermore, if God was not able to protect the Bible from corruption, how can we be certain that he was able to protect the Qur'an from corruption? Did he suddenly acquire new powers which he did not have before?

• Allah must not be perfect and holy. Allah of the Qur'an makes mistakes. It seems that he is still on a learning journey. Since his truth is not regarded as eternal, Allah appears as a fallible being in man's fallen image. Thus, his majesty and stability are not above reproach.

As one follows this logic, it becomes apparent that Allah possesses different characteristics than the God of the Bible. He is manlike in his shortcomings as evidenced by erroneous revelations that he later corrects. The God of the Bible, on the other hand, stands apart as the Holy One whose ways are above human ways and whose perfection, holiness, omniscience, and omnipotence never come into question.

## "Eloi, Eloi, lama sabachthani?"

After the great epic by Mel Gibson, *The Passion of the Christ*, came into theaters, many Muslims were intrigued by Jesus' words on the cross: "Eloi, Eloi, lama sabachthani?" ("My God, My God, why have You forsaken Me?" [Mark 15:34]). What caught people's attention was the similarity of the word *Eloi* with the word *Ilahi*, which also signifies "my God" in Arabic. To those Muslims, Jesus' cry was proof positive that Allah is the God of the Bible, and therefore, we should all follow him.

Linguists tell us that the Arabic word *ilah* was derived from the Aramaic word *eloi*. If Arabic is a sacred and superior language according to the Qur'an, then is it not curious that the Qur'an would use an inferior language (Aramaic) to denote the Creator? Is Arabic, the *lingua sacra* (sacred language) of Islam, such a wanting language that it does not even have a word to describe the Creator?

Muslims pointed to the cry of Jesus on the cross as evidence that Allah is the God of the Bible and that Islam is the true path to him. The irony of this statement, however, is that most Muslims do not believe that Jesus was crucified. Does that mean when it now suits them that Jesus was indeed crucified? But if Jesus was crucified, then God must have had a reason to subject Him to such agony and suffering. Could that reason have been that Jesus was the atonement for the sins of humankind, as promised by God?

## Does Islam Worship the God of Judaism?

If Islam truly worshiped the God of Judaism, as it claims to do, Islam would clearly abide by Judeo-Christian theology that can be summarized as follows:

1. *Humans are sinners and unable to keep the law.* The Qur'an is replete with legalistic rituals that may have well found their origins in the Old Testament. Both Islam and Judaism are two branches of the tree of legalism, as they are both replete with prescribed social, economic, and religious decrees. Legalism puts the burden of salvation in the people's corner, and it builds them up as masters of their salvation. However, if Islam is to learn from Judaism, it will discover that four thousand years of Jewish history taught that humanity is incapable of keeping the Law, and the Law, in turn, is incapable of justifying anyone in the human race.

The Jewish law included moral commands like the Ten Commandments. Because the law is very strict, if a person breaks one of God's commands, that person is guilty of breaking them all. In other words, if a person tells the smallest lie, it is as though he had broken all Ten Commandments. But it's even more serious than that. God is so holy that one can sin with the mind without even carrying out the act (see Matt. 5:27–48), "Anyone who even looks at a woman with lust in his eye has already committed adultery with her in his heart" (Matt. 5:28 NLT).

If all humanity is guilty of sin, can obedience to the law make them innocent? Islam borrowed dietary laws from Judaism, such as abstaining from eating pork. When Jesus' disciples questioned Him about dietary laws, He pointed out that they should not focus on external things but on matters of the heart. Jesus answered them:

> "Are you so lacking in understanding also? Do you not understand that whatever goes into the man from outside cannot defile him because it does not go into his heart, but into his stomach, and is eliminated?" (Thus He declared all foods clean). And He was saying, "That which proceeds out of the man, that is what defiles the man. For from within, out the heart of men, proceed the evil thoughts, fornications, thefts, murders, adulteries, deeds of coveting and wickedness, as well as deceit, sensuality, envy, slander, pride, and foolishness. All these evil things proceed from within and defile the man" (Mark 7:18–23).

**External obedience to the law does not make a person spiritually clean.**

As one can see, external obedience to the law does not make a person spiritually clean.

In addition to the moral and dietary commands, Islam also borrowed other religious customs from Judaism. Here are some instances where Islam freely copied Judaism:[31]

- *The House of God:* In Judaism, the house of God was the temple where God is present. In Islam, the house of God is the Ka'aba where Allah is present.
- *Pilgrimage:* Faithful Jews go to Jerusalem during the festival called Hag on pilgrimages. Muslims go once in a lifetime on pilgrimages to Mecca, called Hajj.
- *Ritual purity:* God commanded the Jews to be consecrated and to wash their garments to be in a state of purity before approaching Him (Exod. 19:10, 11). Muslims ceremoniously wash (ablution) before approaching God with their prayers and wear Ihram (sacred clothing for men) during their pilgrimages.
- *Sexual abstinence:* God commanded the Jews to abstain from women when He appeared to them on Mount Sinai (Exod. 19:15). Muslims observe sexual prohibitions while approaching Allah in Ihram.
- *Forbidden bounds:* Parts of the temple were banned from non-Jews under penalty of death. Muslims forbid non-Muslims from entering the territory of Mecca.
- *Consecration to God:* During a Jewish man's vow of a Nazirite, he was not to shave his head until the seventh day (Num. 6:1–9). While in Ihram, Muslims do not put a razor to their bodies, but during

> If a person cannot keep the law, it follows that the law cannot justify an individual before a holy God.

the ceremony of desacralization, they cut locks of their hair.

- *Sacrifices:* While in consecration, Jews bring offerings to the Lord. While in Ihram (during Hajj), Muslims bring offerings to Allah (the only Muslim sacrifices).
- *The number seven:* God commanded Joshua to circle around Jericho seven times. While on pilgrimage, Muslims are commanded to go around the Ka'aba seven times and to run seven times between al Safa and al Marwa.

The Old Testament contains one story after another of people's disobedience to God's laws. The theme of the Old Testament is that humanity is incapable of keeping God's law. If a person cannot keep the law, it follows that the law cannot justify an individual before a holy God. It's interesting to note that after God gave Moses the Ten Commandments, God commanded Moses to lock them up in a box (ark of the covenant). Two observations can be made from this:

1. The law kills (as one cannot keep it).
2. Since the ark of the covenant symbolized the presence of God, having the law so close to God was an indication of how seriously God values the law.

**2. God offered humanity a gift that is greater than any person's sin.** If God were to allow peoples' sins to go unpunished, He would cease to be God for He would forego His infinite justice and dilute His absolute moral perfection. Since it was impossible for people to keep the law, God offered humankind a way to be justified, not according to one's works, but as a gift:

> Christ redeemed us from the curse of the Law, having become a curse for us, for it is written, "Cursed is everyone

who hangs on a tree"—in order that in Christ Jesus the blessing of Abraham might come to the Gentiles, so that we
would receive the promise of the Spirit through faith (Gal.
3:13, 14).

In his book, *Is Allah the Same God as the God of the Bible?*, M. J.
Afshari defines Allah, "Al-ilah; the god; the supreme; the all-powerful; all-knowing; and totally unknowable; the pre-determiner of
everyone's life destiny; chief of the gods; the special deity of the
Quraish."[53] Note that Allah of Islam retained all the above attributes from its pagan days, especially the fact that Allah is unknowable. There is indeed a major difference between Allah and the
God of the Bible. Allah is distant and removed from humankind.
The God of the Bible, however, is a God of intimacy and personal
relationships. It is the height of blasphemy for a Muslim to call
Allah "father." The God of the Bible, however, loves people so
much that He wants every person to have a personal relationship
with Him and intimately know Him as Father.

**3. That gift, which was incarnate in the Messiah, is called grace.**
Contrary to cultural Islamic belief, Jesus is presented in the Qur'an
as the Messiah. He is described as the Word of God, born of a virgin, the Spirit of God, a sign for humankind, and a mercy from
God. In Surah 3:45, 46 of the Qur'an, the angel said to Mary:

> *O Mary! Allah gives you glad tidings of a Word from Him: his
> name will be Christ (the Messiah) Jesus, the son of Mary, held
> in honor in this world and in the Hereafter and of (the company
> of ) those nearest to Allah. He shall speak to the people in child-
> hood and in maturity. And he shall be (of the company) of the
> righteous.*

The Qur'an even tells of Jesus' resurrection in Surah 19:33, 34: *"So peace is on me on the day I was born, the day that I die, and the day that I shall be raised up to life (again)"! Such (was) Jesus the son of Mary: (it is) a statement of truth, about which they (vainly) dispute.*

> In stripping God from His love toward a fallen humanity, Islam reinvented God into a deity who is far removed from His creation.

Surprisingly, Islam accepted Jesus' miracles. It also accepted Jesus as the Messiah, the fulfillment of the Old Testament. It accepted His virgin birth and the fact that God sent Him with the words of truth. It even alluded to Jesus' resurrection from the dead, as seen in the above quotation. Furthermore, Surah 5:46, 47 of the Qur'an reads:

> *We (God) sent Jesus the son of Mary, confirming the law that had come before him: We sent him the Gospel: therein was guidance and light, and confirmation of the Law that had come before him: a guidance and an admonition to those who fear Allah. Let the People of the Gospel judge by what Allah has revealed therein. If any do fail to judge by (the light of) what Allah has revealed, they are (no better than) those who rebel.*

Islam was ahead of Judaism in recognizing and accepting Jesus as the Messiah. However, Islam gave Jesus the title of Messiah but without the biblical meaning behind it (Matt. 16:15–17; see also Matt. 1:1, 16, 17; 2:4; and John 1:41). The term *Messiah* was never intended to be a hollow label as Islam has made it to be.

Because human beings could not keep the law, nor be justified by it, the God of the Bible gave humanity a gift that was much greater than a person's sin—it was a gift that humankind could never earn. He sent a Savior to save all humankind from the law. The penalty of sin was paid on the cross. The mercy of God is not receiving what one deserves—eternal damnation. The grace of God is receiving what one does not deserve—a glorious heaven.

## The Great Divide

If Muslims believe that Jesus is the Savior whom God sent, then what is the great theological divide between Christianity and Islam? It boils down to substitutionary atonement (a substitute would suffer on another's behalf) and sanctification by blood. The Bible presents God as One who is consumed with His love for humanity. The Messiah is the very expression of God's love to us. "For God so loved the world that He gave His only begotten Son, that whoever believes in Him shall not perish, but have eternal life" ( John 3:16).

In stark contrast, the Qur'an presents a person with a god who is ready to inflict the final punishment (Surah 50:16). The Messiah's mission was to be the innocent Lamb of God whose blood was shed for humankind's salvation. It's no surprise that the Bible contains 342 references to the "blood," the last of which refers to the second coming of Jesus in the book of Revelation:

> And I saw heaven opened, and behold, a white horse, and He who sat on it is called Faithful and True, and in right-eousness He judges and wages war. . . . He is clothed with a robe dipped in blood, and His name is called The Word of God (Rev. 19:11–13).

Even though the Qur'an borrowed liberally from the Bible, it misunderstood the purpose of the biblical Scriptures. This is evident by the absence of the mention of blood as the instrument of redemption in the Qur'an. God said, "Without shedding of blood there is no forgiveness" (Heb. 9:22). God confirmed time after time that sin can never be washed away without the shedding of blood. Blood was the seal of the covenant (Gen. 15:9–21; Heb. 9:11–14). The very word *covenant* means "to cut."

> Although the Qur'an adopted most of its stories from the Bible, it left out the instrument of redemption that the God of the Bible requires.

Although the Qur'an adopted most of its stories from the Bible, it left out the instrument of redemption that the God of the Bible requires.

Muslims balk at the idea of substitutionary atonement by blood. But if the Qur'an comes from the God of the Bible, then where is the blood that God requires for the remission of guilt? Thus, it is clear that instead of continuing and confirming the Judeo-Christian theology, Islam is a complete departure from the principles that the God of the Bible outlined. This leads one once again to ask, has God changed?

It's important to note however that blood does not completely disappear in Islam but becomes marginalized. Muslims celebrate Eed Al-Adha (Feast of Sacrifice), where they sacrifice animals in commemoration of when Abraham was about to slay his son as a sacrifice to the Almighty. In fact, Al Bukhari stated that the prophet Muhammad believed that animal sacrifice was a divinely appointed instrument to receive God's acceptance.[54] Why then do Muslims balk at the idea that the innocent can die for the guilty when their own customs, traditions, and prophet encourage it? Muslims find that Abraham's intended sacrifice on Mount

Moriah was a random incident without meaning. They do not understand that this was a foreshadowing of God sacrificing His own Son on a cross on that same mountain for the salvation of the world.

## Conclusion

God called Abraham out of the idolatrous religion of the moon god because He wanted to reveal Himself to the world through Abraham's descendants. The favorite name of the moon god in the Arabian Peninsula became Allah ("the god"). Arabs were longing for a monotheistic religion of their own, so the moon god Allah became the supreme deity of Mecca prior to Muhammad. Soon, Allah became the generic name of god that the pagans used to refer to their respective deities. When Islam's prophet began his ministry, he superimposed the biblical monotheistic credentials upon the moon god Allah who was dear to the Quraish (prophet's tribe), and presented him as the God of the Bible.

While the Qur'an freely borrowed from the biblical narratives, it reinvented God by stripping Him of His love, His very essence. Thus, the Qur'an marginalized God's grace, compassion, and mercy. Sadly, without comprehending the intensity of God's love and His sacrificial atonement at the cross, Muslims are left with only a handful of legal prescriptions that cannot produce salvation. Jesus counseled that God does not desire legal prescriptions, which no one is able to keep, but He desires grateful hearts that worship Him in spirit and in truth.

In comparing the God of the Bible with Allah, there are irreconcilable differences. It's worthwhile to summarize some of these differences:

- The one (Allah) bears the iconic symbol and religious customs of the pagan moon god from which God called Abraham, while the other (God) is the true God of Abraham.
- The one abrogates his word at will and issues conflicting revelations, while the word of the God of the Bible is eternal, standing the test of time.
- The one is a distant and impersonal god, while the other is the personal heavenly Father who loves us intensely and desires to have a personal relationship with all humanity.
- The one presents a perverted view of the Creator, portraying heaven as a sexual paradise with perpetual virgins, while the other presents a perfect and unpolluted heavenly abode centered on the worship of the Creator.
- The one offers a god who is ready to inflict the final punishment (Surah 50:16), while the other presents a God who took humanity's punishment.
- The one requires meaningless works, while the other requires blood for the remission of sin.

After examining the evidence, one is left with the conclusion that Allah of the Qur'an is as far removed from the God of the Bible as the East is removed from the West.

# SIX

# Are Muslim Customs and Beliefs from God?

*For the whole Law is fulfilled in one word, in the statement,*
*"YOU SHALL LOVE YOUR NEIGHBOR AS YOURSELF." . . .*
*But if you are led by the Spirit, you are not under the Law.*
*Now the deeds of the flesh are evident, which are: . . . enmi-*
*ties, strife, jealousy, outbursts of anger, disputes, dissensions,*
*factions . . . and things like these, of which I forewarn you,*
*just as I have forewarned you, that those who practice such*
*things will not inherit the kingdom of God. But the fruit of*
*the Spirit is love, joy, peace, patience, kindness, goodness,*
*faithfulness, gentleness, self-control; against such things there*
*is no law (Gal. 5:14, 18–23).*

## The Ahadith

Although the Arabic words *Ahadith* and *Sunnah* are used interchangeably when referring to Muslim traditions, there is a difference between the two. The word *Hadith* (pl. Ahadith), is a narration about the life of Islam's prophet including what he approved. The word *Sunnah* on the other hand, depicts how Islam's prophet lived his life as validated by the consensus of his companions (Sahaba). In essence, the Sunnah contains what Muslim scholars consider true from the Ahadith concerning the prophet's life. It is the second source of Islamic jurisprudence after the Qur'an. The Qur'an admonishes Muslims to follow the example of Islam's prophet: *"And whatever the Messenger gives you, take it, and whatever he forbids you, leave it. And fear Allah: truly Allah is severe in punishment"* (Surah 59:7).

Islam is engineered to appeal to the Arabs' way of life, including their love of storytelling and belief in superstition and jinns (spirits). The Ahadith present Muslims with peculiar customs and tales that are neither rational nor defensible, but which have gained a great following due to their shock value. One can never underestimate the impact of the Ahadith in the lives of Muslims. While the Qur'an specifies only three daily prayers (Surah 11:114; 24:58), the Ahadith specify five daily prayers, as well as the five pillars of Islam. The Ahadith also embellish the prophet Muhammad in ways not envisaged in the Qur'an. While the Qur'an offers no attested miracles of Islam's prophet, the Ahadith recount many purported miracles of his, including splitting the moon (*Sahih Bukhari*, vol. 5, bk. 58, no. 209; vol. 5, bk. 58, no. 208; vol. 6, bk. 60, no. 387; vol. 4, bk. 56, no. 831). The Ahadith also reports an instance when the prophet Muhammad purportedly invoked the rain (vol. 8, bk. 73, no. 115).

But what accounts for Muhammad's extreme makeover in the Ahadith? Why do the Ahadith recount many miracles that he supposedly performed, while the Qur'an clearly claims that its development is the only miracle of Islam? This glaring inconsistency between the Qur'an and the Ahadith is explained by the fact that early Muslims gained prestige, power, and financial rewards by producing the Ahadith. Soon afterward, a whole industry churned out a large mass of purported Muhammadan miracles that found no support [isnad] in the Qur'an.

As a consequence, the Sunnah and Ahadith tried to portray the lofty side of Islam's prophet as the perfect example for Muslims to emulate. However, if the man, Muhammad, is the model, wouldn't that indicate that Islam is made in man's image? Furthermore, if Islam is in man's image, then how could it possibly be eternal?

## Pious Monkeys, Urine Ingestion, and Sexual Demigods

The following is one of the more shocking stories in the Ahadith of *Sahih Bukhari*:

> *Some people of 'Ukl or 'Uraina tribe came to Medina, and its climate did not suit them. So the prophet ordered them to go to the herd of [Milch] camels and to drink their milk and urine [as a medicine]. So they went as directed and after they became healthy, they killed the shepherd of the prophet and drove away all the camels. The news reached the prophet early in the morning and he sent [men] in their pursuit and they were captured and brought at noon. He then ordered to cut their hands and feet [and it was done], and their eyes were branded with heated pieces of iron. They were put in "Al-Harra" and when they asked for water, no water was given to them. (vol. 1, bk. 4, no. 234).*

The glaring inconsistency between the Qur'an and the Ahadith is explained by the fact that early Muslims gained prestige, power, and financial rewards by producing the Ahadith.

The following details in this story are troubling. First, the pagan prescription of drinking camel's urine for medicinal purposes, second, the barbarity and lack of any hint of mercy in this incident with the branding of eyes, the cutting off of hands and feet, and leaving people to scorch under the hot sun without water. This is one of the most authenticated stories in the Ahadith of *Sahih Bukhari*, as it is repeated twelve times (isnad). However, the inconsistencies in these twelve accounts of the same story provide a glimpse of the inaccuracy and unreliability of the Ahadith:

- The men were from Ukl in five instances (vol. 4, bk. 52, no. 261; vol. 7, bk. 71, no. 623; vol. 8, bk. 82, no. 794; vol. 8, bk. 82, no. 796; and vol. 9, bk. 83, no. 37).
- The men were from Uraina in two instances (vol. 2, bk. 24, no. 577; vol. 8, bk. 82, no. 795).

Henri Lammens attempts to explain the rampant inconsistencies in the Ahadith:

It [the Ahadith] is a heterogeneous composition made up of elements that are for the most part apocryphal and often contradictory. This type of literature can shock us, and why not? The Muslim student is not worried by historical synthesis. His intellectual effort does not rise above analysis, which is always purely external! He does not let himself question its intrinsic credibility. In his view, the Hadith has, above all, theological value, invoked to support isolated doctrines.[1]

While the Qur'an offers only the assurance of salvation to martyrs, the Ahadith offers several conflicting ideas on the assurance of salvation. In one instance, the prophet said that those who guarantee him the chastity of their private parts and their tongues will be guaranteed paradise (*Sahih Bukhari*, vol. 8, bk. 82, no. 799). In another instance, the prophet said that whoever "believes in Allah and his Apostle, offers prayer perfectly and fasts during the month of Ramadan, will rightfully be granted Paradise by Allah, no matter whether he fights in Allah's cause or remains in the land where he is born" (*Sahih Bukhari*, vol. 4, bk. 52, no. 48). In one place, it guarantees paradise to martyrs (vol. 1, bk. 2, no. 35), while in another instance it says, "Whosoever will meet Allah without associating anything in worship with Him will go to Paradise" (vol. 1, bk. 3, no. 131). Elsewhere, one learns that "whoever prays the two cool prayers ('Asr [early morning] and Fajr [early evening]) will go to Paradise" (vol. 1, bk. 10, no. 548). Yet in another place, the Ahadith claim that "whoever offers prayers perfectly five times a day, observes fasts during the month of Ramadan, and pays the Zakat [obligatory charity] will be successful [i.e., be granted paradise]" (vol. 1, bk. 2, no. 44).

> The Muslim student is not worried by historical synthesis. His intellectual effort does not rise above analysis, which is always purely external!
> —Henri Lammens

These assurances seem whimsically dispensed without forethought. If a person satisfied only one of the conditions listed in one of the Ahadith but not the others, what would be his or her fate? In other words, if a person who prays two cool prayers and remains an idolater, would he still enter paradise? If the person believed in Allah and his apostle, yet did not guard the chastity of his private parts or tongue, would he still enter paradise? As one can see, the formula for entering paradise is not clear. Since Islam does not make sense without interpretation, Muslims have to help

Allah out by explaining what Allah really meant to say. However, who is to say they have the right interpretation given that the authors themselves are confused? Thus, in the Ahadith, truth seems to vary in color much like a chameleon. Truth seems to be fluid, constantly changing.

> In Islam, truth is not constant, but it seems to constantly vary.

Some notations in Ahadith seem to be strange and outlandish. They fit more for shock value and entertainment than to outline a clear path for piety. For instance, male chauvinism has a prominent place in the Ahadith. In one Hadith, the prophet commented on the Persians crowning the daughter of Khosrau as their ruler, by saying: "Such people as ruled by a lady will never be successful" (vol. 5, bk. 59, no. 709). Several Ahadith also present Muslims with rules about defecation. They should not face or turn their backs to the Qibla (direction of prayer to Mecca), but they should either face east or west (vol. 1, bk. 8, no. 388). Another strange custom is Islam's prophet's command, "If a fly falls into the vessel of any of you, let him dip all of it [into the vessel] and then throw it away, for in one of its wings there is a disease and in the other there is healing [antidote for it], i.e., the treatment for that disease" (vol. 7, bk. 71, no. 673).

Ahadith give an eyewitness account of male monkeys surrounding a she-monkey, during the pre-Islamic period of ignorance [jahiliyya], and stoning it because it had committed illegal sexual intercourse. In the story, the observer also assisted the monkeys in stoning the she-monkey (vol. 5, bk. 58, no. 188).

Thus, these stories from the Ahadith rain questions: Are women unfit to lead? Does God keep a record of when and how people answer the call of nature? Do flies contain an illness in one wing and a cure in another? Could monkeys stone a homosexual monkey because of their piety?

Furthermore, according to six Ahadith, King Solomon had relations with all his wives one evening so they would conceive and give birth to knights who would fight in Allah's cause. An angel told Solomon to say, "If Allah wills it." However,

> Some notations in Ahadith seem to be more fit for shock value and entertainment, than to outline a clear path for piety.

since Solomon neglected to say these words, only one wife conceived, but she gave birth to a half-man. The prophet Muhammad said, "If Solomon had said: 'If Allah wills,' Allah would have fulfilled his desire and that saying would have made him more hopeful" (vol. 7, bk. 62, no. 169). It is interesting that the number of Solomon's wives differs from one rendering of the story to another: varying from one hundred wives, to ninety-nine, to ninety, to seventy, and then to sixty (vol. 7, bk. 62, no. 169; vol. 4, bk. 52, no. Number 741; vol. 8, bk. 78, no. 634; vol. 8, bk. 79, no. 711; vol. 9, bk. 93, no. 561; respectively). Whatever the correct number may be, is it conceivable that Solomon had relations with between sixty to one hundred wives in one night?

Many Ahadith were invented and sold for profit in the early days of Islam, which explains the outlandishness and unreliability of the texts. Thus, the Ahadith contain stories of pious monkeys, urine ingestion, and sexual demigods. It is difficult to see any redeeming

> Many Ahadith were invented and sold for profit in the early days of Islam, which explains the outlandishness and unreliability of the texts.

value in these outlandish stories that are designed to captivate the fertile imaginations of Arabs.

## Islam and the Doctrine of Jihad

The events of September 11, 2001, raise fundamental questions in the West concerning the basic religious tenets that Muslims are called to obey. While the majority of Muslims are peace-loving people who want the same basic things that Americans want—liberty and the pursuit of happiness—a small Islamic fundamentalist fringe has made its program of violence and terrorism heard in the West. What is troubling, however, is that this fundamentalist fringe gets its war cry from "holy writings."

Islamic scholar Abdul Saleeb states: "It's not true that Christians have been nice and Muslims have not. But when Muslims engage in violence, murder, and other acts of terrorism, they can legitimately claim that they are following the commands of God as found in the Qur'an and in the examples of Islam's prophet and his teachings. This represents a major distinction between Christianity and Islam."[2]

As one examines the concept of Jihad in the Ahadith, the Ahadith command Islamic world domination, according to Islam's prophet. This is precisely the Hadith that Osama Bin Laden quoted on the heels of 9/11:

*I have been ordered [by Allah] to fight against the people until they testify that none has the right to be worshipped but Allah and that Muhammad is Allah's Apostle, and offer the prayers perfectly and give the obligatory charity, so if they perform that, then they save their lives and property from me except for Islamic laws and then their reckoning [accounts] will be done by Allah (vol. 1, bk. 2, no. 24).*

As a result, when Muslim extremists inflame the West with their terror rhetoric, they do so in faithfulness and obedience to their prophet. According to Islam's prophet, even stones will aid in the jihadists' quest: *"Allah's Apostle said, 'You [Muslims] will fight with the Jews 'til some of them will hide behind stones. The stones will [betray them] saying, 'O 'Abdullah [i.e., slave of Allah]! There is a Jew hiding behind me; so kill him'"* (vol. 4, bk. 52, no. 176).

When confronted with the above Hadith or with any Qur'anic surahs concerning fighting those who do not believe in Allah, Muslims living in the West typically point out the peace-loving Meccan revelations. These include Surah 2:579 which claims there is no compulsion in religion or Surah 24:45 which says to dispute only kindly with Jews and Christians. Most Muslim scholars, however, agree that the fanatic Medinan revelations which were revealed when Muhammad gained many adherents and became strong militarily, abrogated (cancelled) the earlier peace-loving verses when Islam's prophet was weak in Mecca. Despite this fact, Muslims use the abrogated Meccan verses to suit their purposes, when they feel the need to present Islam as a religion of peace.

Even though most Muslims present Islam as a religion of peace, the terrorists who carried out the attacks on 9/11 in New York and Washington, the terrorists who beheaded Americans Nick Berg and Paul Johnson in Iraq, the terrorists who killed teachers, parents, and schoolchildren in North Ossetia, Russia, and the terrorists who carried out the suicide bombing at a Muslim wedding in Amman, Jordan, were following the Qur'an. They are on a Jihad to fight against people until all people acknowledge that "none has the right to be worshiped but Allah and that Muhammad is Allah's apostle." For jihadists to believe that they are doing God a favor by slaughtering the innocent is a tragic and heartbreaking misunderstanding of God.

It's dreadful that the cold-blooded murdering thugs who commit such abominations believe that God will reward their satanic deeds by placing them in paradise. Jesus said "by their fruit you will recognize them" (Matt. 7:16). Their fruits do not edify a holy God, but the prince of darkness. Can anyone in clear conscience call this evil good? Jihad is against every conscience, ethic, and moral code the Creator has embedded in the fabric of the human soul. Thus, jihadists offer themselves as sacrifices on the altar of darkness. Yes, paganism is alive and well in the world today, for the moon god demands sacrifices on his altar.

> To think that the jihadists believe they are doing God a favor by slaughtering the innocent is a tragic and heartbreaking misunderstanding of God.

Listed below are some Qur'anic verses that Jihadists use to justify their actions. Though most Muslims do not heed its call, fighting is actually prescribed in the Qur'an. In fact, the Qur'an contains sixty-four specific calls to fight, including:

- *Fighting is enjoined on you, and is an object of dislike to you; and it may be that you dislike a thing while it is good for you, and it may be that you love a thing while it is evil for you, and Allah knows, while you do not know (2:216).*
- *Fight them, Allah will punish them by your hands and bring them to disgrace, and assist you against them and heal the hearts of a believing people (9:14).*
- *And kill them wherever you find them, and drive them out from whence they drove you out, and persecution is severer than slaughter, and do not fight with them at the Sacred Mosque until they*

*fight with you in it, but if they do fight you, then slay them; such is the recompense of the unbelievers* (Surah 2:191).

- *Fight those who do not believe in Allah, nor in the latter day, nor do they prohibit what Allah and His Apostle have prohibited, nor follow the religion of truth, out of those who have been given the Book, until they pay the tax in acknowledgment of superiority and they are in a state of subjection* (9:29).

- *You who believe, fight those of the unbelievers who are near to you and let them find in you hardness; and know that Allah is with those who guard [against evil]* (9:123).

- *Surely Allah loves those who fight in His way in ranks as if they were a firm and compact wall* (61:4).

- *The punishment of those who wage war against Allah and His apostle and strive to make mischief in the land is only this, that they should be murdered or crucified or their hands and their feet should be cut off on opposite sides or they should be imprisoned; this shall be as a disgrace for them in this world, and in the hereafter they shall have a grievous chastisement* (5:33).

It's difficult to imagine how a religion can become a license to hatred, barbarity, and debauchery (see Mark 12:29–31). Though major religions may disagree in their understanding of God, most however understand the Creator as a force of good instead of evil, love instead of hatred, and holiness instead of iniquity. God does not command the world to come to know Him by force while people's hearts are far from Him (see Matt. 15:8), for He cares about the attitude of the heart (15:19).

According to the Qur'an itself, which carries greater authority than the Ahadith, salvation is not guaranteed for the Muslim except in the case of martyrdom for those who fight for Islam. The Muslim heaven that awaits these martyrs was designed for men since sensual mermaids of heaven are expected to fulfill their every wish.

Heaven, however, is all about God, His holiness, His majesty, and His grace. It's not about crass animalistic behavior. The greatest, indescribable pleasure that one will ever attain is to be in the presence of the Almighty. A glimpse of God's presence will dwarf a person's wildest imaginations. Heaven is not a sexual orgy, but it's the abode of a holy God. The Muslim concept of a sexual paradise presents a perverted view of the Creator, for would a holy God partake in such animalistic behavior? If not, then why would He surround Himself with it?

## Is There Compulsion in Islam?

The Qur'an claims that there is no compulsion in Islam (Surah 2:256). Compulsion is the opposite of free will, self-determination, and liberty. Compulsion implies legalism, oppression, force, coercion, obligation, constraints, and duress instead of heartfelt actions. Perhaps, the hijab (veil) that Muslim women wear in Saudi is the best example to illustrate the concept of compulsion. If women were forced to wear the hijab, that would imply that there is compulsion, but if they had the free will to decide for themselves whether to wear it or not, then that would imply the absence of compulsion.

Despite Muslim assertions that there is no compulsion in Islam, it's ironic that women in Saudi Arabia, the seat of Islam, are forced to wear the hijab, even though the hijab is not mentioned in the Qur'an. The value of a woman in fundamentalist Muslim regimes, such as in Saudi Arabia, is the same value as a pair of shoes. They cannot show up in courts, drive cars, or wear red on Valentine's Day. They are banned from sciences, sports, and arts. By law, they must abide by the seventh-century dress code of the prophet's wives. Fifteen women who tried to escape a school fire in Saudi without their legal attire were forced to go back into the flames to retrieve their appropriate dress covering, and died as a result.[3]

Shiites (the second largest Muslim denomination) in Saudi are viewed as the products of a Jewish conspiracy aimed to divide Islam. Consequently, they cannot be represented in Saudi courts, or be appointed to the bench in the birthplace of Islam. Furthermore, Saudi leaders, who outlaw any Christian activity on their soil, asked President George H. W. Bush, the Commander in Chief of the United States Army, not to pray during Thanksgiving with his troops who were defending Saudi Arabia from none other than a Muslim army (Iraq's). A newspaper columnist in Nigeria invoked the name of Christ without any retribution, but several weeks later when he made a disrespectful comment about the prophet Muhammad during the 2002 Miss World Beauty Pageant, his offices were set ablaze. Al-Jazeera reporters in Saudi, Kuwait, Jordan, and Iraq who dared to criticize the regimes of those countries were expelled as a result. Eighty-seven percent of Muslims who are non-Arabs are forced to read the Qur'an and pray in a language (Arabic) they cannot understand.[4] Muslims must by law pray five times a day or risk being whipped by the morality police in Saudi. Muslims all over the world dare not ask their mullahs self-inquiring questions about Islam.

Furthermore, the black Muslim Sudanese have been victims of ethnic cleansing by means of genocide, rape, and slavery by the janjaweed militia (Arab Muslim Sudanese) because they do not subscribe to the strict code of shari'a law that the government of Sudan would like to impose on them.[5] Christian churches are bombed in Baghdad on Sunday.[6] Millions of Muslims face "honor killing," such as the father of fourteen-year-old Nuran Halitogullari in Turkey, who strangled his daughter with a wire to restore the family's honor after she was kidnapped and raped.[7] Ex-Muslims who dared become Christians have been executed throughout the centuries by the prophet's command.[8]

Are not these things the fruits of evil compulsion?

Islam's autocratic, self-righteous, violent actions find no room for dialogue or the free exchange of ideas. Islam has no room for self-examination, critical analysis, earnestness, and sincerity. It demands violence, coercion, and the hijacking of free will under the guise of peace and non-compulsion. Islam fuses animism into monotheism and insists on having its followers become religious automatons who worship and conform by force instead of by heartfelt convictions. In Islam, self-inquiry is treated as a cancer that must be forcefully removed and terminated. Freedom of speech and democracy are considered to be evil, Western vices that have no place in Islam. To follow Muhammad means to execute those who dared oppose him. Thus, in Islam, a good Muslim obeys without questioning, without thinking.

Compulsion has been a major feature of fundamentalist Islamic regimes. It's no wonder then that the grandson of Ayatollah Khomeini fled Iran to Najaf after the American liberation of Iraq. Hussein Khomeini, who publicly lent his support to the students and reformists in Iran, claimed that Iran needed democracy and the separation of religion and state. He called Iran's Islamic republic the world's worst dictatorship. But why did this leading Shiite cleric flee the so-called Islamic utopia of Iran? "Because freedom is more important than bread," says Khomeini, whose uncle, Ahmad Khomeini, was assassinated when he stopped supporting the Iranian regime and publicized his opposition to it.[9] If there is no compulsion in Islam, then why do Islamic countries such as Saudi Arabia, Iran, Taliban Afghanistan, and Sudan deny their populations freedom, which is "more important than bread"? Why do they force them to be religious automatons that must do as they are told and are denied the basic rights of self-evaluation, critical thinking, and self-determination?

Those who dare to question the mullahs are condemned to death for blasphemy like university professor Hashem Aghajari in Iran. Aghajari's crime was that he stood for "an Islam that brings about freedom and is compatible with democracy and human rights." Aghajari dared to suggest that people should not slavishly follow hard-line interpretations of Islam.[10]

No rational defense can support the claim that there is no compulsion in Islam. Rather, Islam spews coercion, intimidation, and oppression from its every crevice. Its values do not support freedom of expression, pluralism, and multiculturalism. Instead, it seeks to command automatons whose mental faculties are shackled to a seventh-century way of life that does not tolerate freedom of expression. Under the shadow of the caliph Al-Ma'moun's court before freethinking was snuffed out in Islamic circles, Al Kindy wrote: "Religion and the civil power are, in the Muhammadan system, so welded together, that the Iaesa Majestas ["injured majesty"] of the State is ever ready to treat an attack on Islam as high treason of an unpardonable stamp."[11]

> Islam produces automatons whose mental faculties are shackled to a seventh-century way of life that does not tolerate freedom of expression.

## A Life of Futility

In Greek mythology, Sisyphus offended the gods of the pantheon when he revealed secrets of the immortal to mere mortals. As punishment, he was condemned to repeat the process of rolling a massive stone to the top of a hill, only to watch it roll down. The life of Sisyphus was consigned to futility.[12] Although Sisyphus was a fictional character, he is an archetype of a pointless life. In like manner, it is indeed tragic that millions of Muslims blindly follow the edicts and pillars of their religion without the assurance of everlasting life.

The Qur'an discusses the scales of justice on the Day of Judgment that determine whether individuals have earned places in heaven or not: *"Then those whose good deeds are heavy, those are the successful. And those whose good deeds are light, those are they who have lost their souls, abiding in hell"* (Surah 23:102, 103).

Author Ravi Zacharias summarized people's relationships with God in Islam effectively when he said:

In Islam, the distance between God and humanity is so vast that the "I" never gets close to the "Him" in God. And because this distance between the two is impossible to cross, worship takes on an incredible clutter of activity, designed to bring the worshipper close. Repetition and submission take the place of the warmth of a relationship. One only need glimpse a Muslim at worship to see the difference.

> It is indeed tragic that millions of Muslims blindly follow the edicts and pillars of their religion without the assurance of everlasting life.

Yet, with all that he observes and all the rules he keeps, there is never a certainty of heaven for the common person in Islam. It is all in the will of God, they say. One's destiny is left at the mercy of an unknown will. When relationship is swallowed up by rules, political power and enforcement become the means of containment. . . . In the Christian message, the God who is distinct and distant came close so that we who are weak may be made strong and may be drawn close in communion with him, even while our identity is retained.[13]

The Qur'an asserts that people are sinners; even Islam's prophet was not immune to sin (see Surah 47:19; 48:2). The question is, however: Can a person atone for his own sins? If so, then does that person not require a Savior (Messiah)? In order to answer this question, one must explore the meaning of sin. Holiness is an attribute of the transcendent Almighty God, and sin is the opposite of holiness. Thus, when one sins, that person is rebelling against God's nature and everything He stands for. Sin is metaphorically raising one's fists to the Creator of the universe and challenging His holiness. God takes sin seriously. No wonder Satan was cast out of heaven and Adam and Eve were expelled from the garden as a result of sin.

Psalm 130:3 (HCSB) says: "If you, Lord, should mark iniquities, O Lord, who could stand?" Since God is holy, any sin, no matter how small, is a rebellion against His holy character. For God to allow sin to go unpunished is to compromise His holy character. Moreover, since the act of sin is against God Himself, only God can forgive sin. The above passage continues: "But with You there is forgiveness" (v. 4. HCSB). Since sin is rebellion against God's holiness, it follows that only He can forgive us. Furthermore, the Bible tells us that the wages of our sin is death (Rom. 6:23). Therefore, God sent the Messiah to bear the punishment for humanity's rebellion so that His forgiveness could be available to everyone.

R. C. Sproul states:

> It all comes back to our understanding of the character of God. If God is holy, and He measures my sin against His holiness, it would be impossible to even balance the scales. . . . The question raised by historical Judaism is: What human being could possibly survive the perfect judgment of a perfect God? If God is perfectly just, how can I—as an unjust person, with my iniquities—stand that judgment? . . . As long as we can keep the character of God in eclipse and can conceal from our vision who He is, we can continue to flatter ourselves that we can balance the scales of justice or earn our way into the kingdom of God. This is the greatest human delusion there is.[14]

Although Muslims have a form of godliness, they have no spiritual power. They do not have the assurance of eternal life because the Qur'an never promises it. Even the prophet Muhammad prayed for the forgiveness of his sins on his deathbed. In like manner Abu Bakr, the caliph who succeeded the Muhammad, was so insecure concerning his salvation that he wished he'd never been born.[15] Since the Qur'an guarantees salvation only to martyrs (Surah 3:157, 158, 169–171, 195), is it any wonder then that Islam developed a frightening new vocabulary?

> If God is holy, and He measures my sin against His holiness, it would be impossible to even balance the scales.
> —R. C. Sproul

- fatwas (religious decree)
- suicide bombers
- shari'a (Islamic jurisprudence)
- jihad (religious war)
- mujahedeen (religious warriors)

Is it any wonder then that Islam sanctions carnage and butchery in the name of Allah while they turn around and call Allah merciful and compassionate?

R. C. Sproul summarizes the Muslim quest to attain salvation: "If we simply trust in doing our best, our best will only get us into hell; our best is simply not good enough. My assurance is based on Christ's best, on what He has done for us."[16]

## Conclusion

If Muslims were to model their lives according to the Ahadith, they would have to resort to the medicinal virtue of a mixture of camels' urine and milk. They would have to guard the chastity of their private parts to enter paradise; to listen closely to hear stones betraying where Jews are hiding so Muslims can kill them; to conquer the world with the sword for Islam; to refrain from electing women as rulers; and to never defecate while facing north or south. If a fly falls into a cup, they are to dip both wings of the fly into the vessel. Although Islam markets itself as a natural religion of reason, the Ahadith throw all natural reason to the wind.

Islam never addresses the root cause behind the fall of Adam and Eve from the Garden of Eden even though that event broke people's fellowship with the Creator. Islam, however, simply presents an instruction book on how to live, while the cancer of sin is still lurking, metastasizing, and waiting to consume eternal life.

To follow the pillars of Islam is like rolling a massive stone to the top of a hill, only to watch it roll down. It's an exercise in futility, much like the life of Sisyphus.

Sin is a horrible malignant cancer of the soul for which there is no human cure. Muslims underestimate people's sinfulness and God's holiness. They believe that by simply following their religious pillars, they are on Al Surat al mustaqeem (the straight path), for they say (the five Islamic pillars of faith):

1. We believe in one God [shahada], but God says: "You believe that God is one. You do well; the demons also believe and shudder" (James 2:19).
2. We pray five times a day [salat], but God says: "So when you spread out your hands in prayer, I will hide My eyes from you; yes, even though you multiply prayers, I will not listen" (Isa. 1:15).
3. We give to charity [zakat], but God says: "Store up for yourselves treasures in heaven, where neither moth nor rust destroys, and where thieves do not break in or steal" (Matt. 6:20).
4. We fast during the month of Ramadan [sawm], but God says: "When they fast, I am not going to listen to their cry" (Jer. 14:12).
5. We go on pilgrimage at least once in a lifetime [hajj], but God says of the man-made structure in Mecca, which they encircle during hajj, and which they believe is like a structure in heaven: "You shall not make for yourself an idol, or any likeness of what is in heaven above" (Exod. 20:4).

So if Muslims follow their religious pillars listed above, would that make them good? God tells us that all have fallen short of the glory of God (Rom. 3:23) and that "there is no one who does good, not even one" (Ps. 53:3). The Pharisees during Jesus' day studied the Old Testament and followed thousands of religious rules, but Jesus condemned them because their worship was inwardly focused. They put their trust in their own strength instead of in God, and, by so doing, they exalted themselves. God's Word says, "Everyone who exalts himself will be humbled, but he who humbles himself will be exalted" (Luke 18:14).

# SEVEN

# The Finale

*"Like a jewel's brilliance is displayed on a black cloth, Jesus'
love is displayed against the blackness of sin, and the filth of
the flesh."*

—CHARLES R. SWINDOLL[1]

## To Stone or to Forgive???

In his investigative-journalistic book, *The Case for
Christ,* Lee Strobel cites the famous psychological pro-
filer, John Douglas. Douglas was publicly credited by
Oscar nominee Jodie Foster for his invaluable assistance in
the making of the film, *Silence of the Lambs.* Douglas examined all the evidence and clues left behind to understand
human behavior and deduce an individual's psychological
makeup. In an interview with *Biography* magazine, he
declared: "Behavior reflects personality."[2]

If behavior reflects personality, a whole book could be
written concerning the human behavior and psychological
profiles of the two main personalities in Christianity and
Islam. In so doing, one would uncover the motivations that
drove these two sacred giants. But one simple story can lend
insight into the hearts and minds of these two great men so

that one can uncover the DNA strands of their respective personalities. After all, comparison is the beginning of all serious scholarship.

The same story, the same plot, and players consisting of a holy man, a mob of bloodthirsty accusers, and the accused repeated itself over half a millennium apart. The plot is about two women caught in adultery and brought before these two sacred men. The accusers bore stones, ready to inflict the ultimate punishment. In each case, the men bearing stones asked: "What should we do with her?"

In both instances, the men involved believed that the adulterers were transgressing the laws of God in an evil way. After all, weren't these women evil and their vices the epitome of sin? Shouldn't they be stoned?

Muslim tradition recounts that when the prophet Muhammad was in the Oasis of Khaybar, Sonic Jews brought a Jewess caught in the act of adultery. They asked him what they should do. The prophet Muhammad asked for a copy of the Torah and had the Law of Moses read that states that the adulteress should be stoned, so Muhammad simply ordered her to be stoned.[3] In Islam, obedience to the Law comes before everything.

Some six hundred years earlier, scribes and Pharisees brought a woman caught in the act of adultery to the temple where Jesus was teaching ( John 8:1–11). Jacques Jomier eloquently summarized this encounter:

> To embarrass Jesus, the defenders of morality ask him what they should do. It is a trap. The Law is formal: it calls for stoning. Jesus does not contradict the Law; he is simply scornful of the accusers, who are so hard on this woman and so lacking in shame for themselves. "Let him who is without sin

cast the first stone!" says Jesus, and everyone leaves in silence, one after another. Jesus is far from approving the act of which the woman is accused. He calls sin sin, and evil evil, when he tells the woman: "Go and sin no more."[4]

No sooner had Jesus spoken His words of truth than the would-be stoners loosened their grips from the stones they had held so tightly moments earlier. Blinded by the light of His words and the compassion of His spirit, they hung their heads in shame and faded away. Those who came to trap Jesus were outclassed and silenced. They knew that the woman was undeniably guilty, but one encounter with Jesus made them realize that they, too, were guilty. This encounter with Jesus helped them recognize that they were no different than the adulteress, for the Law said that if they had broken one command, they had broken the whole Law.

In essence, the would-be stoners were also adulterers and in bondage to sin in the eyes of God. They were murderers, liars, idolaters, and blasphemers. Jesus was the only one who could condemn the adulteress because he was sinless, but the sinless one chose to forgive. This story provides deep insights into Jesus' mission. He did not come to condemn but to forgive. He did not come to liberate with the sword but to liberate with His blood and by the power of His love. As such, the one who hated sin had an undying love for sinners.

> Jesus was the only one who could condemn the adulteress because he was sinless, but the sinless one chose to dispense grace.

The one (Jesus) forgives; the other (Muhammad) stones. The one loves; the other assaults. The one embraces the sinner; the other repels her. These are a symphony of contrasts, the thesis and antithesis, antidote and poison, redemption and judgment standing side by side, each beckoning for an embrace.

Those in the presence of Muhammad were made to be proud. They had no need for grace, for they trusted in their own hands to save them. Lacking mercy they stoned the adulteress. On the other hand, Jesus' light humbled those who were in His presence. They realized their sinfulness. They understood their true natures. They did not judge, lest they be judged, assault lest they be assaulted, or repel lest they be repelled. The realization of their own sins produced compassion for others, so they forgave.

> Jesus did not come to liberate with the sword but to liberate with His blood and by the power of His love. As such, the one who hated sin had an undying love for sinners.

Jesus never made apologies for sin—He knows that sin is in our hearts (see Matt. 15:19, 20). In fact, He came to redeem humanity from sin in order to restore a broken relationship with God. Jesus said to the woman's accusers, "He who is without sin among you, let him be the first to throw a stone at her" (John 8:7), and mercy was dispensed. But in Islam, judgment is unrelenting as the decision belongs to the Law.

Jomier states concerning the story of the adulteress: "Here we find two basically different attitudes to life, to human beings and to God, corresponding to the different demands of the two respective dogmas," one that believes in the law and which stones and the other that believes in grace and forgives. Jomier continues: "Jesus' authority, his goodness, and his firmness are striking: he acts as a teacher of the Law and his forgiveness far exceeds that of other men." Jesus saw the bigotry of man, and thus, instructed His followers not to judge, lest they be judged (Matt. 7:1). Jesus had a more realistic consideration of the wretchedness of human nature as illuminated by the Old Testament, which shows men and women subject to congenital weakness.[5]

Jesus saw the duality of sin and bigotry in our hearts. That is why He came. That is why He died. That is why He rose from the dead. Islam did not see it. I hear the words in that Shakespearian play: "The fault, dear Brutus, lies not in the stars, but in ourselves." In the same way, sin lies not in external influences and intruding factors, but it lies within us, in our hearts, which are separated from a holy and perfect God. God's perfection demands that justice for our sin be served. Therefore, instead of becoming gods in our own eyes and pridefully trusting in our bankrupt righteousness to save us, we need to humble ourselves and trust in the righteousness of God. We need to be like Abraham, the believer, who believed by faith, and whose faith—not works—was credited to him as righteousness.

## The Case

Because I did not always exist, it follows that I had a beginning. If I had a beginning, I must also have an end. Therefore, I am finite. If I am finite, my wisdom, intellect, and righteousness suffer the same deficiency. Thus, it is absurd to propagate the myth that the finite can produce a metaphysical (non-normal) attribute of the infinite. Only the infinite is morally perfect. Since we are not eternal, our limited understanding is therefore incapable of encompassing moral perfection. The only way for us to commune with God would be for God to compromise His holiness by allowing our moral imperfection into His presence. But how is it possible for our imperfections to coexist for eternity with God's moral perfection?

Darkness and light cannot coexist, for one will subdue the other. To believe that our imperfections can coexist with God's morally transcendent, infinite, and eternal perfection is to strip God of His holiness and make Him sinful like we are. The finite can never become infinite; we can never become God. Thus, only the infinite can produce moral perfection. What is finite (humans) can never become transcendent (going beyond the limitations of time and space) in order to produce moral perfection. To believe that we can in fact achieve moral perfection is blasphemy. However, where we have failed, God Himself made a

> **In order to save us, God the Son became one of us, without ceasing to be God; and He was called the Son of God.**

way. The infinite can wear a finite shell (human body), but He cannot lose His infinite essence. Thus, in order to save us, God the Son became one of us, without ceasing to be God; and He was called the Son of God.

The Qur'an did away with God's grace and made people into gods who could attain righteousness despite their finitude. Thus in Islam, people spend their lifetimes following laws designed for achieving eternal life, without even the slightest assurance from Allah that their efforts would be rewarded. In Islam, Muslims blindly follow the pillars without the slightest assurance of salvation, "for in Islam only Allah knows."

Islam says, "Simply follow the pillars." But when people simply follow the pillars (the Law), they move away from faith and dependence on God to faith and dependence on themselves.

Christians thank God for their salvation. Muslims, however, would thank themselves in the impossible event that the scales were to tip in their favor. If one decodes the implications, the message of Muslims is: "It's all about me. Who needs God?" Thus, by following the pillars of religion, without addressing the problem of sin in their lives, Muslims are missing the whole point. They are not addressing the real problem that separates sinners from a holy God. They do not see their need for repentance. When one recognizes their sins, they sense a need for repentance. Muslims do not deal with the problem of sin, but they become like religious robots, who legalistically pray five times a day, but whose hearts are vile and filled with unconfessed and unrepented sin.

Legalistic religious pillars are not the answer, for they can never make one clean in God's sight. They do not address the matters of the heart from whence evil comes and which makes us unclean (see Mark 7:18–23). When we measure our works—prayers, fasting, and almsgiving—we sin against the Almighty because we set our sights on ourselves instead of on Him. By legalistically measuring our works, we become proud, arrogant, and boastful. We become our own gods; hence the Scripture reminds us: "For by grace you have been saved through faith; and that not of yourselves, it is the gift of God—not as a result of works, so that no one may boast" (Eph. 2:8, 9).

Salvation is not about how great a person is, how much they contribute, or how much they perform, but it is all about God and

Him alone. Sin, on the other hand, enthrones and focuses the spotlight, as it were, on one's self instead of God. Satan rebelled because he wanted to be as God. Likewise, Cain did not want to follow God's ways and became guilty of innocent blood. Pridefully, he said to himself, "God, I have a better way." King David was filled with the pride of life. He ordered Joab to take a census against the Lord's wish because he wanted to see how great he was. "Look at me, look at all my people, look at all of my kingdom's wealth, oxen, sheep, and cattle. Look at how great I am." But in doing so, he became proud and sinned against the Lord.

> Legalistic religious pillars are not the answer, for they can never make us clean in God's sight.

Similarly, because of the pride of life, Arabs are reputed to have said, according to the Qur'an, "Send us a prophet of our own people and in our own language, and we will follow him." Thus, they were not interested in salvation except to say to their neighbors, "Look, we too have a prophet and a religion of our own." That is the epitome of the pride of life. It is inconsistent with God's character to presume that God provides the Arabs one path, the Jews another, and the non-Semitic yet another. Truth is eternal and for multiple truths to exist would negate the universality and eternality of truth and make it relative.

Plato said: "The philosopher is in love with truth; that is, not with the changing world of sensation, which is the object of opinion, but with the unchanging reality which is the object of knowledge."

> Sin enthrones and focuses the spotlight, as it were, on one's self instead of God.

Relative truth is a lie because truth is eternal, transcending the time-space capsule of our human experience. An old adage says: "If it's new, it's not true, because truth is eternal." Therefore, it is inconceivable that God revealed a new truth to Islam's prophet when truth was already revealed through the biblical prophets concerning the Messiah.

Moral absolutes have no place in the Qur'an. Allah of the Qur'an seems like a vacillating deity who cannot make up his mind as he issues contradicting revelations. By principle of deduction, the Qur'an implies that God's character is changing, that He is not immutable, and that He cannot make up His mind. Again, by deduction, the Qur'an infers that God's ethics are situational, that His righteousness can be compromised, and that His holy character falters. That, however, would be a god in our fallen image. That kind of god without moral absolutes is not worth worshiping.

> **Truth is eternal and for multiple truths to exist would negate the universality and eternality of truth and make it relative.**

God manifested His grace through His Son, Jesus Christ, so that the whole world—peoples of every race, culture, and creed—will come to know Him. He said, "For by grace you have been saved through faith; and that not of yourselves, it is the gift of God; not as a result of works, so that no one may boast" (Eph. 2:8, 9). God created us for His pleasure, and to say that He desires our works is to make Him shallow, but God is infinitely more profound than that. He desires love and gratitude from our hearts. Thus, the pillars of Islam become instruments of self-righteousness, of people boasting in themselves and their own accomplishments instead of the Creator's.

To trust in religious pillars to save a person is like believing that God's holiness has a price tag or that it can be bought by a handful of deeds. However, where humanity could not make a way, God did. A transaction occurred when the Messiah came and was crucified as God promised in the Torah (Pentateuch) and the Zabur (Psalms) to pay for our sins.

## The Trial

In a court of law, it is incumbent on both the accuser and the defendant to appeal to the highest principles of reasonable persuasion in either introducing or attacking evidence. Legal codes declare that evidence is relevant when it has a tendency in reason to prove or disprove disputed facts. Having served on a jury, I learned that the defendant's objective was to create reasonable doubt that he was guilty. In other words, the counsel representing the defendant does not have to prove the innocence of the accused but to create reasonable doubt in the minds of the jurors that the defendant was guilty.

> The pillars of Islam become instruments of self-righteousness, of people boasting in themselves and their own accomplishments instead of the Creator's.

In like manner, if Islam were on trial today, all one would have to do to disprove that it is the religion of the Almighty is to establish reasonable doubt in the minds of the jurors. This book drew on the principles of reasonable persuasion and presented deathblow after deathblow to tenets of Islamic faith, including Allah, the prophet Muhammad, the Qur'an, the customs, and the human condition [fitrah].

The verdict: Islam self-destructs before the flames of critical analysis.

## The Evidence

*People.* Concerning people, Muslims believe that Adam's sin affected him alone, and that humans are born in a pure state until they commit guilty deeds. The Qur'an confirms that all have sinned and gone astray from the straight path (Surah 1:5). Even the prophet Muhammad purportedly prayed seventy times a day that Allah would forgive his sins. The only question is whether one can achieve moral perfection on his/her own, or whether he/she requires a Savior. If Adam could cover his own sins, then he would have found himself back in the garden. But the very fact that Adam and his descendants were confined to lives of work, sweat, illness, and death is a nagging reminder that the effects of sin are real and that humans cannot negate them with their works. Islam, however, trivialized the seriousness of sin and did not address the very cancer that ate at a person's soul and separated him from God.

> To trust in religious works to save us is like believing that God's holiness has a price tag or that it can be bought by a handful of deeds.

The Bible states that if one commits the smallest sin, then that person has become an enemy of God (Rom. 5:6–10). Therefore, all

> If Islam were on trial today, the verdict would be served: Islam self-destructs before the flames of critical analysis.

of a person's works, praying, fasting, and pilgrimages could not save him. All these religious activities cannot atone for a person's sins. In the whole of the Qur'an, only Jesus Christ is depicted as sinless (Surah 19:19). By God's grace, the great chasm between Adam (man) and God was bridged by a Savior covered in blood and crowned with thorns. Only His blood can get you and me into God's holy presence.

*The Qur'an.* Unfortunately, Muslims are taught to accept their canons without the benefit of rational inquiry and scientific examination. Although the Qur'an claims to be divinely inspired, it is unsystematic and is full of scientific, grammatical, historical, and textual errors. It has contradictions, incoherencies, imperfections, plagiarisms, pagan influences, discrepancies, fallacies, and abrogation. The notion that the Qur'an is heavenly in origin is intellectually embarrassing.

The enmity subsisting between different Muslim caliphs who had a hand in putting the Qur'an together such as Ali and Abu Bakr, as well as Omar and Uthman, is well known. Each of these caliphs entered into the text whatever favored their own claims, and left out what did not. How, then, can a person distinguish between the genuine and the counterfeit? Uthman was called the "Tearer of the Books," as he burned all other copies of the Qur'an. Two hundred verses have been abrogated or cancelled by additional verses that transcribers thought better. This translates to 3 percent of the Qur'an openly acknowledged as false. Thus, it's not surprising that caliph Ma'moun ridiculed the idea that the Qur'an was uncreated.

Furthermore, the Dome of the Rock, Islam's third holiest shrine, indicts the inerrancy of the Qur'an and refutes the claim that the Qur'an was not changed, as it contains inscribed Qur'anic passages in its structure that are divergent from the modern Qur'an.

*The Prophet Muhammad.* The prophet Muhammad was a prophet-king seduced by luxury, women, riches, and affluence instead of an ascetic biblical prophet who set his sight on the Creator and the afterlife. He died as the largest landowner in the Arabian Peninsula. Muhammad led many wars, assassinated his enemies, and performed no substantiated miracles. He lost wars, was injured in a war, and was poisoned by one of his victims, which hastened his death. Furthermore, Islam's prophet had no witnesses to attest to his purported ascension to heaven.

Al Kindy offered the following dilemma to his Hashimite friend:

> Thy Master [Muhammad] reiterates emphatically that he was "sent with mercy to the whole human race." Mercy, in slaying, plundering, and enslaving! . . . Thou art never weary of crying up thy faith as divine; and anon [now] thou turnest clean round, and sayest just the opposite; for what, after all, are these doings—killing and shedding of blood, raping and robbery, and making slaves of men and women—what are they, but the works of the Devil?"⁶

Muhammad's view of religion was vastly different from that of Jesus. The actions of Islam's prophet could certainly not be reconciled with the command that Jesus laid down, which is to love one's neighbors like oneself. Shouldn't the fruits of a prophet of the Almighty be mercy, benevolence, and brotherhood instead of bloodshed?

*Allah.* Having examined firsthand historical and archeological evidence, one concludes that Allah is not the God of the Bible. Instead, he is the pagan moon god whom Abraham and his family worshiped before they worshiped the Creator, YHWH. Allah was later worshiped as one of 360 deities in the pagan pantheon in Mecca along with his daughters, Al-Lat, Al-Uzza, and Manat during the days of the prophet Muhammad. Allah was the chief deity in the pantheon with his iconic crescent moon that later became the symbol of Islam. In order to appease the Meccans, Islam's prophet originally sanctioned the worship of the daughters of Allah along with Allah via a Qur'anic revelation. However, after his followers objected, the prophet Muhammad rescinded these "satanic verses," by claiming they were given to him by Al Shaitan (Satan).

The Bible states that "God is not a man, that He should lie" or change His mind (Num. 23:19). However, the Allah of the Qur'an does not seem omniscient but he is manlike in his characteristics since he makes mistakes that he later corrects (Surah 2:106).

Perhaps the most striking difference between the eternal God of the Bible and Allah of the Qur'an is that the former exhibits an intense love for people and wants them to be His sons and daughters. Conversely, it is blasphemous for the Muslim to refer to Allah as a heavenly father. In reality, the moon god was given an extreme makeover in Islam and presented as the biblical monotheistic God.

***Customs.*** What good are Islam's pillars if they are powerless to guarantee salvation? It's futile to follow a set of rules when a person knows they will not provide the assurance of salvation. Although the Ahadith are entertaining, they are also troubling. It is puzzling how stories of monkeys stoning monkeys, as well as people ingesting camels' urine, or performing amazing sexual feats as featured in the Ahadith could pertain to one's spiritual enlightenment. Furthermore, it defies reason that diabolical, murdering jihadists are duped into believing that by killing the innocent, they are rewarded with seventy-two virgins for a sexual orgy in paradise.

Although Islam markets itself as a natural religion of reason, the Ahadith throw all natural reason to the wind. Surprisingly, Muslims are not troubled by historical synthesis of the Ahadith. The glaring inconsistency between the various Ahadith is explained by the fact that early Muslims gained prestige, power, and financial rewards by producing the Ahadith.

Muslims defend the purity of their scriptures and assert that "Islam is a religion, born in full light of history." Henri Lammens comments:

> So many authorities have repeated this claim that, when we go back to the origins of the movement and we come across "fiddling" everywhere, we cannot help but be disconcerted. Disappointment is followed by a vague annoyance as we start to examine the pseudoscientific apparatus, all the iron-mongery [hardware] of the Isnad [chain of narrators who contributed the Hadith], and the variants and the editorial tricks destined to conceal this primitive machinery.[7]

**Summary.** Upon examining the evidence of the prophet Muhammad, the Qur'an, Allah, as well as Muslim customs and beliefs, it becomes apparent that the Islamic set of beliefs does not reconcile with the Bible unless one waters down the holiness of God. It's astonishing that over a billion Muslims in the world blindly follow Islam without first investigating the unholiness of their god, the errors within their scriptures, the feet of clay of their founder, the hopelessness of their followers, and their bizarre and eccentric customs.

The revolutionary step that Islam took in bringing monotheism to the pagans in the Arabian Peninsula was not revolutionary enough. Islamic thinking only unveiled part of the truth but kept the other parts hidden that speaks of God as a God of love and compassion instead of wrath. Yes, God is One. He is from everlasting to everlasting, but God is also holy and God is love. It is His will for none to perish but for all to come to know Him (see 2 Pet. 3:9). The mere knowledge of His oneness does not begin to address His holiness. It does not bridge the unbridgeable and wash unclean hearts from wickedness; for that, humankind needs a

Savior. Though Islam pointed to Jesus as the long-awaited Messiah, Islam ignored Jesus' shed blood for the remission of sins.

But had there been another way to salvation besides the cross, such as Islam, God would never have allowed the Messiah to suffer such an agonizing death. The late Adrian Rogers said it best: "That's why Jesus stepped out of the glories of heaven, and walked the dusty shores of Galilee. That's why Jesus left heaven's love for earth's abuse. That's why Jesus was nailed to that hellish machine called the cross and died in agony and blood. Why? With every drop of His blood, He's saying: 'I love you and I want to save you.' He's saying: 'Stop. Don't go to hell.' "[8]

Jesus Christ said: "I tell you the truth, whoever hears my word and believes him who sent me has eternal life and will not be condemned; he has crossed over from death to life" ( John 5:24 NIV). According to the Savior, those who realize they are sinners, repent of their sins, and receive Him as Savior and Lord are "born again" ( see John 3:3–5).

I f the Holy Spirit is moving upon your heart and you want to receive Jesus Christ as Savior and Lord of your life, then simply:

- Acknowledge that you are a sinner,
- Repent of your sin,
- Tell Jesus that you receive him as Lord and Savior in your life,
- Ask Him by faith to come into your life to forgive your sin and give you eternal life.

*Karl Barth, famed theologian, was once asked, "What is the greatest thought you ever had?" His answer: "Jesus loves me this I know, for the Bible tells me so."*

—DALE GALLOWAY, *Rebuild Your Life*

# Appendix

The following is a contrast between the diverse dogmas of Islam and Christianity. I will thus be following the maxim of TV's Sergeant Friday effectively adopted by Ronald Reagan: "Just the facts, ma'am":

| *Jesus* | *Muhammad* |
|---|---|
| **Birth** | |
| Born of a virgin (even according to Qur'an) around 4 BC in Bethlehem | Born of Aminah around AD 570 in Mecca. |
| Jesus Christ's (the Messiah's) birth and coming were foretold in 333 prophecies in the Bible, hundreds of years prior to His birth. Of these prophecies, 456 specific details of His life are given. God gave the Old Testament to the Jews so they would recognize the coming of the Messiah, the Savior of the world. Jesus fulfilled all prophecies foretold of | There are no prophecies concerning the coming of Islam's prophet.

Islam's prophet did not have a forerunner. His coming was not anticipated. He simply claimed to be a messenger of God. |

| Jesus | Muhammad |
| --- | --- |

### Birth

the Messiah in minute detail, during
His birth, miracles, crucifixion,
death, and resurrection.

The angels announced His birth
to the shepherds. John the Baptist
(the forerunner) announced
His coming. The angel Gabriel
announced His birth to Zechariah,
Mary, and Joseph. The Magi came
from the East with gifts to
worship Him.

### The Messiah

"Therefore the Lord Himself will give you a sign: Behold, a virgin will be with child and bear a son, and she will call His name Immanuel [God with us]" (Isa. 7:14, written around 700 years before Christ).

"We gave Jesus the son of Mary clear (signs) and strengthened him with the holy spirit" (Surah 2:87).

"And the angel [Gabriel] said to her, 'Do not be afraid, Mary; for you have found favor with God. And behold, you will conceive in your womb, and bear a son, and you shall name Him Jesus. the Hereafter and of (the He will be great and will be called the Son of the Most High; and the Lord God will give Him the throne of His father David; and He will reign over the house of Jacob

"Behold! The angels said: 'O Mary! Allah gives you glad tidings of a Word from Him: his name is Christ Jesus, the son of Mary, held in honor in this world and to Allah; He shall speak to company of) those nearest the people in childhood and in maturity. And he shall be (of the company) of the righteous" (Surah 3:45, 46).

| *Jesus* | *Muhammad* |
| --- | --- |

forever, and His kingdom will have
no end.' And Mary said to the angel,
'How can this be, since I am a virgin?'
And the angel answered and said to
her, 'The Holy Spirit will come
upon you, and the power of the
Most High will overshadow you;
and for that reason the holy Child
shall be called the Son of God' "
(Luke 1:30–33).

"For the Law was given through
Moses; grace and truth were
realized through Jesus Christ.
No one has seen God at any
time; the only begotten God who
is in the bosom of the Father,
He has explained Him"
( John 1:17, 18).

"And a voice came out of the
heavens: 'You are My beloved Son,
in You I [God] am well-pleased"
(Mark 1:11).

"You are My Son, Today I [God] have
begotten You" (Ps. 2:7). "For God
so loved the world, that He gave
His only begotten Son, that whoever
believes in Him shall not perish,
but have eternal life" ( John 3:16).

"I kept looking in the night visions,
and behold, with the clouds of heaven
One like a Son of Man was coming,

"We [God] sent Jesus the
son of Mary, confirming
the Law that had come
before him: We sent him
the Gospel: therein was
guidance and light, and
confirmation of the Law
that had come before him: a
guidance and an admonition
to those who fear Allah"
(Surah 5:46).

Allah did not confirm
Muhammad's ministry in a
public manifestation.

| Jesus | Muhammad |
| --- | --- |

### The Messiah

and He came up to the Ancient
of Days and was presented before
Him. And to Him was given
dominion, glory and a
kingdom, that all the peoples,
nations and men of every
language might serve Him. His
dominion is an everlasting
dominion which will not pass
away; and His kingdom is one
which will not be destroyed"
(Dan. 7:13, 14, written
centuries before Christ).

"I [God] will also make You a
light of the nations so that My
salvation may reach to the end
of the earth" (Isa. 49:6, written
centuries before Christ).

"Christ the son of Mary was no
more than a Messenger"
(Surah 5:75a).

"For a child will be born to us, a
son will be given to us; and the
government will rest on His shoulders;
and His name will be called
Wonderful Counselor, Mighty God,
Eternal Father, Prince of Peace"
(Isa. 9:6, written around 700 years
before Christ).

"For there is one God, and one
mediator also between God and
men, the man Christ Jesus"
(1 Tim. 2:5).

| Jesus | Muhammad |
|---|---|
| "Then Jesus again spoke to them, saying, 'I am the light of the world; he who follows Me will not walk in the darkness, but will have the light of life' " (John 8:12). | "[I have come to you], to attest the Law which was before me. And to make lawful to you part of what was [before] forbidden to you; I have come to you with a Sign from your Lord. So fear Allah and obey me" (Surah 3:50). |
| "She will bear a Son; and you shall call His name Jesus, for He will save His people from their sins" (Matt. 1:21). | "To you, We (God) sent the Scripture in truth, confirming the Scripture that came before it" (Surah 5:48). |
| "My judgment is true; for I am not alone in it, but I and the Father who sent Me" ( John 8:16). | "And there is none of the People of the Book but must believe in Him before his death; and on the Day of Judgment He will be a witness against them" (Surah 4:159). |

### The Prophet Muhammad

There is no mention of another prophet after the Messiah; on the contrary, the Bible concludes with these stern and uncompromising words: "I testify to everyone who hears the words of the prophesy of this book: if any one adds to them, God will add to him the plagues which are written in this book" (Rev. 22:18).

"Allah and His Angels send blessings on the prophet: O you that believe! You send blessings on him, and salute him with all respect" (Surah 33:56).

| Jesus | Muhammad |
|---|---|

### Titles

| Jesus | Muhammad |
|---|---|
| Door to heaven | An Apostle |
| Eternal life | A Messenger |
| Judge of the living and dead | Son of Abd Allah |
| Messiah (Savior) | A Preacher |
| Prince of Peace | Prophet with the Sword |
| Word of God | A Warner |
| King Eternal | Evangelist |
| First and Last | Seal of the Prophets |
| Bread of Life | The Prophet of Islam |
| Immortal God | Mortal Man |

### Marriage

| Jesus | Muhammad |
|---|---|
| Never married or had relations with any woman. | Married 15 women, including the then seven-year-old Ayisha. |

### Worldly Desires and Riches

| Jesus | Muhammad |
|---|---|
| Jesus was not of this world, nor did He have worldly desires or riches. He said in Matthew 8:20, "The foxes have holes and the birds of the air have nests, but the Son of Man has nowhere to lay His head." | The prophet Muhammad was poor but became well-to-do upon marrying Khadija, his first wife who was fifteen years his senior. He also profited from the booties of war. Ayisha, the youngest of the prophet's wives, used to say that the prophet loved three things: women, scents, and foods. During his wars, the prophet claimed 15 percent of the booty. |

### Great Prayers

| Jesus | Muhammad |
|---|---|
| Jesus taught His followers to pray in this way:"Our Father who is in heaven, Hallowed be | This prayer is called the "Fatiha," or the opening of the Qur'an, which is its first chapter: "In the |

| Jesus | Muhammad |
|---|---|
| Your name. Your kingdom come. Your will be done, on earth as it is in heaven. Give us this day our daily bread. And forgive us our debts as we also have forgiven our debtors. And do not lead us into temptation, but deliver us from evil. For Yours is the Kingdom and the power and the glory forever, Amen" (Matt. 6:9–13). | name of Allah, Most Gracious, Most Merciful. Praise be to Allah, the Cherisher and Sustainer of the Worlds; Most Gracious, Most Merciful; Master of the Day of Judgment. You do we worship, and Your aid do we seek. Show us the straight way. The way of those on whom You have bestowed Your Grace, those whose (portion) is not wrath, and who do not go astray" (Surah 1). |

### Miracles

| | |
|---|---|
| Miraculous birth of Jesus by a virgin as God promised (even acknowledged by the Qur'an). Jesus healed the sick, the blind, and the paralytic, walked on water, rebuked the storms, raised the dead, rose from the dead just as He promised, and as it was foretold by the prophets of old. He appeared to over 500 followers following the resurrection. He performed countless other miracles. Then he was lifted up into heaven in front of His disciples forty days after His resurrection. | The prophet Muhammad claimed that the Qur'an is the Muslim miracle, and issued a challenge in Surah 2:23 for unbelievers to produce a similar Surah to what is in the Qur'an. |

### War and Peace

| | |
|---|---|
| Never lifted a sword. | Proselytized with the sword in sixty-six recorded battles. |

| Jesus | Muhammad |
| --- | --- |

### War and Peace

"Then Jesus said to him: 'Put your sword back into its place; for all those who take up the sword shall perish by the sword' " (Matt. 26:52). (on

"Therefore, when you meet the unbelievers (in fight), smite at their necks; at length until you have thoroughly subdued them, bind a bond firmly them)" (Surah 47:4).

"Blessed are the peacemakers, for they shall be called sons of God" (Matt. 5:9).

"Fighting is prescribed for you, and you dislike it. But it is possible that you dislike a thing which is good for you, and that you love a thing which is bad for you. But Allah knows and you know not" (Surah 2:216).

"You have heard that it was said, 'YOU SHALL LOVE YOUR NEIGHBOR and hate your enemy.' But I say to you, love your enemies and pray for those who persecute you" (Matt. 5:43, 44).

"And fight them on until there is no more tumult or oppression" (Surah 2:193a).

"In everything, therefore, treat people the same way you want them to treat you, for this is the Law and the prophets" (Matt. 7:12).

"Allah only forbids you, with regard to those who fight you for (your) Faith, and drive you out of your homes, and support (others) in driving you out, from turning to them (for friendship and protection). It is such as turn to them (in those circumstances), that do wrong" (Surah 60:9).

| *Jesus* | *Muhammad* |
| --- | --- |
| "Whoever forces you to go one mile, go with him two" (Matt. 5:41). | "And slay them wherever you catch them, and turn them out from where they have turned you out" (Surah 2:191). |
| "You have heard that it was said, 'an eye for an eye, and a tooth for a tooth.' But I [Jesus] say to you, do not resist an evil person; but whoever slaps you on your right cheek, turn the other to him also. If anyone wants to sue you and take your shirt, let him have your coat also" (Matt. 5:39, 40). | "We ordained therein for them: 'Life for life, eye for eye, nose for nose, ear for ear, tooth for tooth, and wounds equal for equal.' But if anyone remits the retaliation by way of charity, it is an act of atonement for himself. And if any fail to judge by (the light of) what Allah has revealed, they are (no better than) wrong-doers" (Surah 5:45). |
| "Let your light shine before men in such a way that they may see your good works, and glorify your Father who is in heaven" (Matt. 5:16). | "Let those fight in the cause of Allah who sell the life of this world for the Hereafter. To him who fights in the cause of Allah, whether slain or gets victory— soon shall We give him a reward of great (value)" (Surah 4:74). |
| "Peace I leave with you; My peace I give to you; not as the world gives do I give to you" (John 14:27). | "Fight and slay the Pagans wherever you find them, and seize them, beleaguer them, and lie in wait for them in every stratagem (of war)" (Surah 9:5). |

| Jesus | Muhammad |
|-------|----------|

### War and Peace

"Behold, I send you out as lambs in the midst of wolves" (Luke 10:3).

"Beware of the false prophets, who come to you in sheep's clothing, but inwardly are ravenous wolves. You will know them by their fruits" (Matt. 7:15).

"You have heard that it was said, 'you shall love your neighbor and hate your enemy.' But I say to you, love your enemies and pray for those who persecute you, so that you may be sons of your Father who is in heaven; for He causes His sun to rise on the evil and the good, and sends rain on the righteous and the unrighteous. For if you love those who love you, what reward do you have? Do not even the tax collectors do the same? If you greet only your brothers, what more are you doing than others? Do not even the Gentiles do the same? Therefore you are to be perfect, as your heavenly Father is perfect" (Matt. 5:43–48).

"Fight in the cause of Allah those who fight you, but do not transgress limits; for Allah does not love transgressors" (Surah 2:190).

"The punishment of those who wage war against Allah and His Messenger, and strive with might and main for mischief through the land is: execution, or crucifixion, or the cutting off of hands and feet from opposite sides, or exile from the land: that is their disgrace in this world, and a heavy punishment is theirs in the Hereafter" (Surah 5:33).

| *Jesus* | *Muhammad* |
|---|---|

### Enemies

Loved his enemies.

Killed his enemies.

### Kingdom

Kingdom not of this world.

Established an earthly empire.

### Law vs. Grace

While Jesus was teaching at the temple, the Pharisees brought before Him a woman caught in adultery, and they inquired of Jesus what they should do in order to test Him and find grounds to accuse Him. They reminded Him that the Law of Moses calls for the stoning of such women. This was a classic trap. The Law is formal: it calls for stoning. Jesus did not contradict the law nor approve of the sin. On the one hand, He is scornful of the accusers, who are filled with pride, and says to them: "Let him who is without sin among you, let him be the first to throw a stone at her."

And He watched them leave in silence. On the other hand, Jesus calls sin sin and evil evil when he told the woman to sin no more (see John 8:1–11).

In the Muslim tradition, there is also an incident when an adulteress is brought before the prophet Muhammad as he was in the oasis of Khaybar. Sonic Jews brought before him a woman caught in the act of adultery. They asked him what they should do, so he called for a copy of the Torah. Since the Torah formally stated that the adulteress should be stoned, he ordered her to be stoned. In Islam, obedience to the Law comes before everything.

| Jesus | Muhammad |
|-------|----------|

### Law vs. Grace

Implication: Mercy is dispensed resulting in grace, which forgives. Jesus taught His followers in Matthew 7:1 not to judge, lest they be judged.

Implication: Judgment is unrelenting, resulting in the Law which stones.

### Foremost Commandment

"One of the scribes came and . . . asked Him, 'What commandment is the foremost of all?' Jesus answered, 'The foremost is, "Hear, O Israel! The Lord our God is One Lord; and you shall love the Lord your God with all your heart, and with all your soul, and with all your mind, and with all your strength." The second is this, "You shall love your neighbor as yourself." There is no other commandment greater than these' " (Mark 12:28–31).

"Say: He is Allah, the One and Only; Allah, the Eternal, Absolute; He begets not, nor is He begotten; And there is none like unto Him" (Surah 112:1–4).

### Salvation

"Jesus said to him, 'I am the way, and the truth, and the life; no one comes to the Father but through Me' " ( John 14:6).

"Those who believe (in the Qur'an), and those who follow the Jewish (Scriptures), and the Christians and the Sabians, and who believe in Allah and the Last Day, and work righteousness, shall have their reward with their Lord: on them shall be no fear, nor shall they grieve" (Surah 2:62).

| Jesus | Muhammad |
|---|---|

### Death

| | |
|---|---|
| Condemned no one to death. | Condemned many to death. |
| Died in Jerusalem at age of 33 by crucifixion. | Died in Medina at age 62, due to pneumonia and poisoning. |
| Arose from the dead on the third day as prophesied and appeared to hundreds of witnesses. | Lingers in his grave. |

### Last Words

| | |
|---|---|
| Jesus never asked for forgiveness for His sins for He was perfect. But one of His last statements on the cross was to forgive those who crucified Him: "Father, forgive them; for they do not know what they are doing" (Luke 23:34). Jesus' last words on the cross fulfilled a prophesy from Psalm 31:5 when He said: "Father, into Your hands I commit My spirit" (Luke 23:46). | The last words of the prophet Muhammad in a whisper were, "Lord grant me pardon; eternity, in Paradise! Pardon. The blessed companionship on high." |

### Second Coming

| | |
|---|---|
| Jesus' second coming is revealed in both the Bible and the Qur'an. He will come to judge (John 5:25, 27). | "And (Jesus) shall be a Sign (for the coming of) the Hour (of Judgment); therefore have no doubt about the (Hour), but you follow Me: This is a straight Way" (Surah 53:61). |

# Glossary of Terms

**Abd-Allah**  The name of Muhammad's father. Literal translation is "a slave of Allah."

**Ablution**  Necessary ceremonial act of cleansing which Muslims must undergo before approaching Allah with their prayers. Muslims must wash the face, feet, hands, ears, arms, and other bodily regions prior to prayer recitation and prostrations.

**AH**  After Hijrah—the dating of Islam. The Hijra, which is the emigration of the prophet Muhammad from Mecca to Medinah, marks the beginning of the Islamic calendar ( July 16, AD 622). The Muslim calendar year is only 354 days long, eleven days shorter than the Western calendar system. This is due to the lunar system used by Muslims, where every year consists of exactly twelve moon cycles. For a Gregorian-Hijrah date converter, please visit: www.islamicfinder.org/dateConversion.php?lang=english.

**Ahadith**  Plural form of Hadith. Traditions relating to the sayings and doings of Islam's prophet. Carries the greatest authority after the Qur'an.

**Ahl al Kitab**   Literal translation is "People of the Book." Refers to Christians and Jews.

**Ahl al-Tawheed**   People of Monotheism—used to refer to Ismailis or Druze sects of Islam.

**Al Kindy**   Christian apologist who served at the court of the caliph Al-Mamum (AD 830).

**Al Massih**   The Messiah (Jesus). This is the Arabic Christian depiction of Jesus. In the Qur'an Jesus is referred to as Isa Ibn Maryam.

**Al Muwahedoon**   The People of Monotheism or Ahl al-Tawheed. Typically refers to Druze sect of Islam which was founded by Al Hakim, the sixth fatimid caliph (AD 996–1021). They believe in reincarnation in order to obtain final purification. They also believe that Hakim will return in the end of days as Al Mahdi (the Savior).

**Al Rahman Al Raheem**   Words used often in the Qur'an to describe Allah. Literal translation is "the compassionate, the merciful."

**Al Shaitan**   Satan.

**Al Surat al mustaqueem**   The straight path. The Qur'an calls this the path of those who do not incur Allah's wrath and who do not go astray.

**Al**   *The* word in Arabic. Was combined with the word *Ilah* (deity) in pre-Islamic times to derive the word *Allah*.

**Allah**   Arabic term for God. Term largely associated with Islam. Allah was one of 360 deities worshiped in pagan mecca prior to

the advent of Islam's prophet. He was worshiped along with
Al-Lat, Manat, and Al-Uzza that were known as the daughters of
Allah.

**Allahu Akbar**   This is the Muslim creed. The literal translation is
"Allah is the Greatest" instead of "Allah is great." Allah was only
one of 360 deities worshiped in Mecca, so one must evaluate this
expression through the polytheistic context that was prevalent in
Muhammad's time. In essence, this expression contrasts Allah with
other deities and asserts that Allah is the greatest of those deities.

**Al-Uzza**   Also known as Asherath and Ashtarout in other parts
of the Middle East and was widely represented by Venus. Pre-
Islamic Arabian fertility goddess who was one of the three chief
goddesses of Mecca. She along with Manat and Al-Lat were known
in Mecca as "the daughters of Allah." She was believed to be a
consort to Baal, the Canaanite god of fertility.

**Ammarah**   The lowest stage in human spiritual development. It
is synonymous with the animal self, when people submit to their
carnal desires like beasts (Surah 12:53).

**Anaza**   A short spear or javelin like the command batons artis-
tically fashioned that the Byzantine government gave to the bar-
barian chieftains who rallied to the Empire. Islam's prophet
carried it at times.

**Arabic**   The liturgical language of Islam. Arabic has been a literary language since at least the sixth century. Muslims are expected
to learn it as they read the Qur'an only in Arabic during worship.

**Asa**   Also known as qadib in Arabic. Literal translation is "stick,"
but it is referenced as a scepter (mihjan) made of precious wood,
encrusted with gold and ivory that Islam's prophet carried.

**Asharite**  Also known as Asha'ri. School of early Muslim philosophy who argued against the Mutazilite school of Greek-inspired philosophers that the comprehension of unique nature and characteristics of God were beyond human capability.

**Asr and Fajr**  Literally translated "early morning." Refers to the required early morning Muslim prayer. It is considered a special prayer along with Fajr (early evening). In fact, there's a Hadith that claims that whoever prays the two cool prayers ('Asr [early morning] and Fajr [early evening]) will go to Paradise."

**Assalum Alaikum**  Muslim greeting. Literal translation is "peace be upon you."

**Ayat**  Qur'anic verses are called ayat.

**Ayoub**  Job.

**Bukhari**  The compiler of the most famous collection of Ahadith by the title of *Sahih Bukhari.*

**Caliph**  A former title for any religious or civil ruler of the Islamic world, claiming succession from Muhammad.

**Cherubim**  Plural of Cherub in Hebrew. High-ranking angels.

**Dawood**  King David.

**Demons**  Demons are considered fallen angels in Christianity. They are one-third of the angels who rebelled with Satan against God.

**Eed**  Religious holiday.

**Eed Al-Adha**  Feast of Sacrifice. Muslim holiday where they sacrifice animals in commemoration of when Abraham was about to slay his son as a sacrifice to the Almighty.

**Fatwa**   Religious decree.

**Fitrah**   The belief that human nature is sound; in other words that people do not congenitally suffer from sin but are born in a pure state.

**Furqan**   The Gospels (the books of Matthew, Mark, Luke, and John).

**Hadith**   Singular form of Ahadith. Traditions relating to the sayings and doings of Islam's prophet. Carries the greatest authority after the Qur'an.

**Hajj**   Pilgrimage. Hajj is the fifth of the Five Pillars in Sunni Islam and one of the ten Branches of Religion in Shi'a Islam. Every able-bodied Muslim who can afford to do so is required to make the pilgrimage to Mecca at least once in his or her lifetime. After this trip, they are called Hajj.

**Hanif**   Believed to be people who held to the "pure" religion of Abraham.

**Hijra**   Emigration. The Hijra was a defining moment in Islam. It occurred in 622 AD when, due to the persecution of the Muslims, the prophet Muhammad joined his followers in an emigration from Mecca, his ancestral homeland, to the welcoming Medina. Qur'anic revelations are divided between pre- and post-Hijra.

**Iblis**   Satan. Also known as al Shaitan in Arabic.

**Ibn Maryam**   Son of Mary.

**Ibrahim**   Abraham.

**Ihram**   Sacred clothing for men which is traditionally worn during their pilgrimages (hajj).

**Ilah**   Means "the deity" in Arabic. Was combined with the word *Al* (the) in pre-Islamic times to derive the word Allah.

**Injeel**   New Testament (Gospels) but can also refer to the entire Bible.

**Isa**   Jesus.

**Isa Ibn Maryam**   Literal translation is "Jesus, Son of Mary." This is the nomemclature used for Jesus Christ in the Qur'an.

**Is-haq (or Is-hac)**   Isaac, son of Abraham (Ibrahim).

**Islam**   Submission or surrender to Allah.

**Isma'il**   Ishmael.

**Ismaili**   The second largest branch in Shi'a community, after the Twelvers who are dominant in Iran. A dispute arose on the succession of the Sixth Imam, Jaafar as-Sadiq. The Ismaili accepted Jaafar's eldest son Ismail as the next Imam, whereas the Twelvers accepted a younger son, Musa al-Kazim.

**Isnad**   Each Hadith contains sanad or isnad, which is the chain of narrators of the Hadith.

**Isra**   Refers to what Muslims regard as Muhammad's miraculous night journey (on night of power) from Mecca to the site of Masjid al-Aqsa (Dome of the Rock) in Jerusalem. It is believed to have been followed by his ascension to heaven (Mir'aj).

**Jahiliyya**   An Islamic concept referring to the spiritual condition of pre-Islamic Arabian society as being in a state of spiritual ignorance.

**Janjaweed**   Arab Muslim Sudanese militia. They have embarked on an ethnic cleansing campaign against other Sudanese by means of genocide, rape, and slavery because they do not subscribe to the strict code of Shari'a law, which the government of Sudan would like to impose on them.

**Jehennam**   Hell.

**Jibra'il**   The angel Gabriel. Purportedly the voice that revealed to the prophet Muhammad that he was chosen to be God's messenger and that gave him the Qur'anic revelations.

**Jihad**   Typically, this word is associated with "holy war" in the West. Muslim scholars however refer to five types of Jihad fi sabilillah (struggle in the cause of God). These are Jihad of the heart/soul (Jihad bin nafs/qalb), Jihad by the tongue (Jihad bil lisan), Jihad by the pen/knowledge (Jihad bil qalam/ilm), Jihad by the hand (Jihad bil yad), and Jihad by the sword (Jihad bis saif).

**Jihad al-akbar**   Literally "the greater Jihad." Spiritual or personal struggle against one's soul (nafs).

**Jihad al-asghar**   Literally translated "the lesser Jihad." Physical struggle against oppressors.

**Jinns**   Spirits—The Arabic term from which the English term Genie was derived.

**Jizya**   Very heavy taxation inflicted on non-Muslims who were under Muslim rule but did not embrace Islam.

**Ka'aba**   Means "House of God." Muslims believe that the Ka'aba was built by Adam on his way out of paradise and then rebuilt by Abraham and Ishmael. Muslims pray facing the Ka'aba (located in Saudi Arabia). They are also commanded to do a pilgrimage there once in a lifetime if able to do so.

**Lawwamah**   The second stage in human spiritual development. It is the self-accusing spirit, the narrowest departure from the narrow path, which rouses the pangs of conscience (Surah 75:2).

**Mahdi**   In Islamic eschatology, al Mahdi (the savior) is the prophesied redeemer of Islam, who will return to change the world into a perfect Islamic society before Yaum al-Qiyamah (Day of the Resurrection).

**Majlis**   Seat. Term used for the seat of Islam's prophet.

**Ma'moun**   (AD 786–833) Muslim caliph who ridiculed the idea that the Qur'an was uncreated.

**Maronite**   Lebanese Christian denomination in full communion with the Pope of Rome.

**Maryam**   Mary.

**Maseeh**   Arabic for Messiah.

**Masjid**   Muslim place of worship. Known in the Western world as a mosque.

**Matn**   The text of the Hadith.

**Minbar**   A pulpit in the mosque where the Imam (leader of prayer) stands to deliver sermons.

**Mir'aj**   Refers to what Muslims regard as the night of power which entails Muhammad's miraculous ascension to heaven following the Isra (trip to Jerusalem). It is celebrated as a holiday in many parts of the Muslim world.

**Mosque**  Muslim place of worship. Known in Arabic as Masjid.

**Muhammad**  Islam's prophet. Muslims refer to him as the seal of the prophets (last of the prophets).

**Mujahedeen**  Also know as Jihadists. Religious warriors—those who take up the call to Jihad.

**Musa**  Moses.

**Mu'tazilites**  Also spelled Mu'tazilite, or Mu'tazilah. Theological school of thought within Islam which originates from the Arabic word "to abandon." They expanded on the logic and rationalism of Greek philosophy, seeking to combine them with Islamic doctrines and show that the two were inherently compatible. They argued during the rule of the Abbasid Khalifate against the Asharites that the Qur'an was created, citing Surah 43:3.

**Mutma'inaah**  The third stage in human development. It is the stage of perfection, when the soul is at rest in perfect peace, having attained the goal of perfection (Surah 89:30a).

**Muttawa**  Generally government-authorized religious police (or clerical police or public order police) that exist within Islamic theocracies. They enforce varied interpretations of Shari'a law, and in which governments are either directly controlled by, or fall significantly under the influence of, Islamic clergy such as in Saudi Arabia.

**Naskh**  Abrogation. Typically appears in the phrase al-nasikh wal-mansukh ("the abrogating and abrogated [verses]"). Naskh typically involves the replacement (ibdal) of an earlier verse/tradition (and thus its embodied ruling) with a chronologically successive one in the Qur'an.

**Pbuh**  Acronym for peace be upon him. Muslims always use these words after they say the name of Islam's prophet. It is a loose translation of the Arabic form (Sallah Allah Alaihi Wa Sallam) which literally translated means "God prays upon him and salutes him."

**Pharisees**  Teachers of the Law—contemporaries of Jesus.

**Qadib**  Also known as Asa in Arabic. Literal translation is "stick," but it is referenced as a scepter (mihjan) made of precious wood, encrusted with gold and ivory that Islam's prophet carried.

**Qiblah**  Direction Muslims face during prayer toward Mecca.

**Quraish**  The tribe of Islam's prophet.

**Qur'an**  The Muslim holy book. Muslims believe that it was revealed to the prophet Muhammad by the angel Gabriel.

**Sabeans**  Pagan cult mentioned favorably in the Qur'an. They admitted the existence of astral spirits and worshiped the stars. Abraham was most likely a Sabean prior to his call and conversion.

**Sahabi**  Plural form is Sahaba. Literal translation is "companion." Term used for Muslims who knew or saw Muhammad, believed in his teachings, and died as a Muslim to be a companion.

**Salam**  Peace.

**Salat**  Prayer. Muslims are called to pray five times a day. This is one of Islam's five pillars.

**Sawm**  Arabic word for fasting which is regulated by the Islamic jurisprudence. It is primarily performed during the Islamic holy month of Ramadan. It is done because of the mandate in the Qur'an, and is considered one of the five pillars of faith.

**Shahada**   The Islamic creed of faith. It is one of Islam's five pillars of faith. It is the declaration of belief in the unity of God (Allah in Arabic) and in Muhammad as his prophet. Recitation of the shahadah is considered one of the five pillars of Islam by Sunni Muslims. When sincerely stated aloud, one is considered to have officially declared oneself a convert to Islam.

**Shari'a**   Muslim jurisprudence. The system of divine law that governs all aspects of life for the Muslims, including religious, economic, political, legal, and social.

**Shi'a**   Also known as Shi'ite. They are the followers of Ali Ibn Abi Talib (Imam Ali). The second largest denomination of the religion of Islam after Sunni. Shi'a Muslims adhere to the teachings of the Islamic prophet Muhammad and his Ahlul Bayt (family). They reject the rule of the initial three Sunni caliphs as Sunnis reject the Imamate of the Shi'a Imams.

**Shirk**   Polytheism, which is Islam's unpardonable sin in Islam. It means "division" in Arabic. It consists of associating partners with God. Due to Muslims' gross misunderstanding of the Trinity, they view it as shirk. The opposite of shirk is Tawhid which asserts the unity of God.

**Suhufs**   Scrolls of parchment on which Uthman's Koran was probably written.

**Sunni**   Largest Muslim denomination. Sunnis are the followers of Abu Bakr and Omar as successors of Muhammad.

**Surah**   Chapter in the Qur'an. There are 114 chapters in the Qur'an, each with a name (e.g., The Fatihah; "The Opening"; Al Baquahah, "The Cow"; etc.).

**Tahrif**   Muslim assertion that the Bible was corrupted.

**Tanzil**   Process of sending down of Islamic revelations. Muslims traditionally believe that the angel Gabriel sent down the revelations to the prophet Muhammad.

**Taurat**   The Law—the books of Moses.

**Tawhid**   Islamic concept of monotheism, derived from Ahad (one). The opposite of Tawhid is shirk, which means "division" in Arabic. Muslims view polytheism and idolatry as shirk.

**The Law**   Term generally used in this book to refer to the Law of Moses in the Bible.

**Torah**   Pentateuch—The Law—the books of Moses in the Bible.

**Ur of the Chaldees**   Also known as Ur of the Chaldeans. Located in the region of Babylon in modern-day Iraq. It is the city from which God called Abraham.

**Uthman ibn Affan**   Third caliph. He reigned from 644 to 656. He is regarded by Sunni Muslims as one of the "Four Righteously Guided caliphs."

**Yahwa(h)**   John the Baptist.

**Yaqoub**   Jacob, son of Isaac (Is-haq).

**Zabur**   Arabic for the book of Psalms in the Bible.

**Zakat**   Arabic word for charity. This is one of Islam's five pillars of faith.

# Notes

## INTRODUCTION

1. Francis Bacon, *Bartlett's Familiar Quotations* ed. John Bartlett (Boston: Little Brown, 1937, 1980), 179.

## CHAPTER ONE
### How I Came to Know Christ as My Savior?

1. Charles R. Swindoll, ed., *Swindoll's Ultimate Book of Illustrations and Quotes* (Nashville, TN: Thomas Nelson Publishers, 1998), 500.

2. The Muslim caliphate Al Hakim ruled from his capital city of Cairo, Egypt. His state extended to the Arabian Peninsula, northern Syria, and most of North Africa.

3. Lebanese Civil War, from Wikipedia, the free Encyclopedia, http://en.wikipedia.org/wiki/Lebanese_Civil_War#Background _to_the_war.

4. Swindoll, *Swindoll's Ultimate Book*, 421.

5. Ibid., 77.

## CHAPTER TWO
### Are People Born in Fitrah? Do They Need a Savior

1. Maulana Muhammad Ali, *The Holy Qur'an with English Translation and Commentary* (Dublin, OH: Ahmadiyya Anjuman Isha'at Islam Lahore, Inc., 2002), 487–88.

2. Ibid.

3. Samy Tanagho, *Glad News! God Loves You, My Muslim Friend* (Waynesboro, GA: Authentic Media, 2003), 158.

4. Ibid. 57.

5. Jack Graham, *Power Point* radio broadcast, 2003.

6. Irshad Manji, *The Trouble with Islam* (New York: St. Martin's Press, 2003), 281.

7. Charles R. Swindoll, *Swindoll's Ultimate Book of Illustrations & Quotes* (Nashville, TN: Thomas Nelson, n.d.), 174.

8. *World Religions: Macmillan Compendium*, Macmillan Library Reference, 1998, New York.

9. R. C. Sproul and Adbul Saleeb, *The Dark Side of Islam* (Wheaton, IL: Crossway Books, 2003), 52.

10. Ibid.

## CHAPTER THREE
## Is the Qur'an the True Word of God?

1. H. A. R. Gibb, *Muhammadanism: An Historical Survey*, 2nd ed. (New York: Oxford University Press, 1955), 25.

2. Ibn Warraq, ed., *The Origins of the Qur'an: Classic Essays on Islam's Holy Book* (Amherst, NY: Prometheus Books, 1998), 9, 10.

3. Ibid., 14.

4. Arthur Jeffery, "Abu 'Ubaid on the Verses Missing from the Koran," in *The Origins of the Qur'an*, 150–53.

5. Ibid.

6. Arthur Jeffery, "A Variant Text of the Fatiha," in *The Origins of the Qur'an*, (New York: Promethus) 145–49.

7. Ibid.

8. Alphonse Mingana, "The Transmission of the Qur'an," in *The Origins of the Qur'an*, 108–9.

9. Ibid.

10. Ibid., 76–96.

11. Ibid., 84.

12. Sahih Bukhari, Hadith, vol. 6, bk. 61, http://debate.org.uk/topics/history/qur_hist.htm.

13. Alphonse Mingana, "Three Ancient Qur'ans," in *The Origins of the Qur'an*, 85.

14. Ibid., 94, 95.

15. Tony Jepson, "Does the Bible or the Qur'an Have Stronger Historical Corroboration?" http://debate.org.uk/topics/history/qur_hist.htm (accessed 26 June 2004).

16. Ibid.

17. William Muir, *The Apology of Al Kindy* (London: Tract Committee, 1887), 27. http://www.muhammadanism.com/Al-Kindi/al-kindi.pdf.

18. Tanagho, *Glad News! God Loves You, My Muslim Friend*, 99.

19. Clinton Bennett, *In Search of Muhammad* (London: Cassel, 1998), 185.

20. Christ's death came at the beginning of the seventy weeks or the end of sixty-nine weeks. "This is checked by noting that 444 BC to AD 33 is 476 years, and 476 times 365.24219 days per year equals 173,855 days. Adding twenty-five days for the difference between March 4 and March 29 gives 173,880 days" Source: The Open Bible—Expanded Edition, New American Standard, Thomas Nelson Publishers. p. 1496.

21. Please note from the text that the Holy Spirit is independent from the angel Gabriel. Gabriel was not claiming that he will fill John, but the Holy Spirit will.

22. Although Gabriel is not mentioned by name in this Scripture, it is presumed to be Gabriel since this is consistent with his appearances to Mary the mother of Jesus (Luke 1:26), and Zacharias, the father of John the Baptist (Luke 1:18, 19) around the same time period.

23. Muhammad's favorite wife Aisha confirmed that he was still lying in bed the whole time this legendary trip through the heavens occurred.

24. W. St. Clair-Tisdall, "The Sources of Islam," in *The Origins of the Qur'an*, 232.

25. Ibid., 288, 289.

26. Muhammadali H. Shakir, *The Qur'an Translation (English Only)*, Tahrike Tarsile Qur'an, 2nd US ed., 1 January 1999, Surah 2:135.

27. St. Clair-Tisdall, "Sources of Islam," 290, 291.

28. Ibid., 235, 6.

29. Ibid., 236, 7.

30. Ibid., 253.

31. Robert Morey, *The Islamic Invasion* (Las Vegas: Christian Scholars Press, 1992), 148.

32. Ibid. 204.

33. St. Clair-Tisdall, "Sources of Islam," 235.

34. Ibid., 255.

35. Morey, *Islamic Invasion*, 148, 149.

36. Ibid., 150.

37. St. Clair-Tisdall, "Sources of Islam," 229.

38. Muir, *Apology of Al Kindy*, 81.

39. Ibid., 44.

40. Ibid., 29.

41. Lafif Lakhdar, Interview with Haaretz, *Religion Within the Limits of Reason*, Memri, www.memri.org, May 5, 2006, Special Dispatch Series No. 1157.

42. Ibid.

43. Ibid.

44. Usama Bin Laden in audiocassette released April 23, 2006, *Arab Reformists Under Threat by Islamists: Bin Laden Urges Killing of 'Freethinkers,'* Memri, www.memri.org, May 3, 2006, Special Dispatch Series No. 1153.

45. Lakhdar, *Religion Within the Limits of Reason.*

46. Muir, *Apology of Al Kindy*, 28, 79.

47. Morey, *Islamic Invasion*, 108.

48. Ibid.

49. Ibid.

50. Ernest Renan, "Muhammad and the Origins of Islam," in *The Quest of the Historical Mohammad*, ed. Ibn Warraq (Amherst, NY: Prometheus Books, 2000), 161.

51. Norman L. Geisler, *Baker Encyclopedia of Christian Apologetics* (Grand Rapids: Baker, 1999), 622.

52. Arthur Jeffery, "The Quest for the Historical Mohammad," in *The Quest of the Historical Mohammad*, ed. Ibn Warraq, 356.

53. Muir, *Apology of Al Kindy*, 79.

54. Mingana, "Transmission of the Qur'an," in *The Origins of the Qur'an*, 77.

55. Anis Shorrosh, *Islam Revealed: A Christian Arab's View of Islam* (Nashville: Thomas Nelson, 1988), 193.

56. Muir, *Apology of Al Kindy*, 68.

57. Geisler, *Baker Encyclopedia*, 625, 626.

58. Ibid., 622.

59. Morey, *Islamic Invasion*, 119.

60. Shorrosh, *Islam Revealed*, 199–200.

61. Mingana, *The Origin of the Qur'an*. 79.

62. Warraq, *The Quest for the Historical Mohammad*, 128.

63. Muir, *Apology of Al Kindy*, 92–93.

64. Ibid., 93.

65. Ibid., 75–78.

66. Ali Sina, "Why I Left Islam," *Islam Review*. Presented by *Pen and the Sword*. http://www.islamreview.com/testimonials/whyileftislam.shtml.

67. Ibn Warraq, *Why I Am Not a Muslim* (Amherst, NY: Prometheus Books, 1995), 115.

68. Geisler, *Baker Encyclopedia*, 624.

69. Morey, *Islamic Invasion*, 50.

70. Geisler, *Baker Encyclopedia*, 624.

71. Karen Armstrong, *Muhammad: A Western Attempt to Understand Islam* (London: Victor Gollanca, 1991), 108–133.

72. Morey, *Islamic Invasion*, 79, 80.

73. Warraq, *Why I Am Not a Muslim*, 114, 115.

74. Statement signed by Sheikh Usamah Bin-Muhammad Bin-Ladin. Text of Fatwah urging jihad against Americans. Published in Al-Quds al-'Arabi, 23 February 1998. http://www.ict.org.il/articles/fatwah.htm.

75. Warraq, *Why I Am Not a Muslim*, 230–3.

76. Josh McDowell, *The New Evidence That Demands a Verdict* (Nashville: Thomas Nelson, 1999), 53.

77. Charles R. Swindoll, ed., in *Swindoll's Ultimate Book of Illustrations and Quotes* (Nashville: Thomas Nelson, 1998), 574.

78. Bennett, *In Search of Muhammad*, 65.

## CHAPTER FOUR
## Was the Prophet Muhammad a Biblical Prophet?

1. Henri Lammens, "Fatima and the Daughters of Muhammad," in *The Quest of the Historical Mohammad,* ed. Ibn Warraq (Amherst, NY: Prometheus Books, 2000), 269.

2. Ibid., 250, 251.

3. Ibid., 251, 252.

4. Ibid., 252–4.

5. Ibid., 249.

6. Ibid., 248.

7. Arthur Jeffery, "The Quest for the Historical Mohammed," in *The Quest of the Historical Mohammed,* 340, 41.

8. Muir, *Apology of Al Kindy,* 49, 50, 52. http://www.muhammadanism.com/Al-Kindi/al-kindi.pdf.

9. Babek Khurramy led a revolt against the caliph Al Ma'moun in Persia around AH 202. He annihilated an entire imperial army. The terror of his name spread in the Muslim empire, as he is said to have slain 250,000 men.

10. Muir, *Apology of Al Kindy,* 45, 46.

11. Sproul and Saleeb, *The Dark Side of Islam,* 92–95.

12. Ibid.

13. Renan, "Muhammad and the Origins of Islam," in *The Quest of the Historical Mohammad,* 133.

14. Ibid., 133, 134.

15. M. H. Shakir, trans., *The Holy Qur'an,* rev. ed., Tahrike Tarsile Qur'an, Inc., 2000. http://www.hti.umich.edu/k/Qur'an.

16. Renan, "Muhammad and the Origins of Islam," 128.

17. Shorrosh, *Islam Revealed,* 252.

18. Renan, "Muhammad and the Origins of Islam," 136.

19. Muir, *Apology of Al Kindy,* 49.

20. Renan, "Muhammad and the Origins of Islam," 138.

21. Sunan Abu-Dawud Hadith, bk. 39, no. 4498; bk. 39, no. 4499. http://www.use.edu/deptMSA/reference/searchhadith.html.

22. Renan, "Muhammad and the Origins of Islam," 142.

23. Shorrosh, *Islam Revealed*, 197.

24. Bennett, *In Search of Muhammad*, 80–82.

25. Hadith, bk. 38, no. 4396.

26. Ibid.

27. Martin Lings, *Muhammad: His Life Based on the Earliest Sources* (Rochester, VT: Inner Traditions, 1987), 341.

28. Jeffery, "The Quest for the Historical Mohammad," 353, 354.

29. Sliman Ben Ibrahim and Etienne Dinet, *The Life of Mohammad—Prophet of Allah* (Secaucus, NJ: Chartwell Books, 1990), 236.

30. Muir, *Apology of Al Kindy*, 62, 63.

31. John 18:36.

32. John 12:28.

33. Matthew 8:20.

34. Matthew 26:52.

35. Matthew 5:16.

36. Jacques Jomier, *How to Understand Islam* (New York, NY: Crossroad Publishing, 1991), 137.

37. John 8:1–11.

38. 2 Corinthians 5:21.

39. Matthew 26:31, 32.

40. John 14:6.

41. Matthew 28:1–7.

## CHAPTER FIVE
## Is Allah the God of the Bible?

1. Muir, *The Apology of Al Kindy*, 17. http://www.muhammadanism.com/Al-Kindi/al-kindi.pdf.

2. Austin Potts, *The Hymns and Prayers to the Moon God*, PhD (Philadelphia, PA: Dropsie College, 1971), 2.

3. Robert Graves, *The Larousse Encyclopedia of Mythology* (New York: Smithmark Publishers, 1960), 54–56.

4. Hafiz Ghulam Sarwar, *Muhammad, the Holy Prophet* (Lahore, Pakistan: Sh. Muhammad Ashraf, 1969), 18, 19.

5. Morey, *Islamic Invasion*, 215.

6. New Covenant Ministries, *The True Origin of 'Allah': The Archaeological Record Speaks, Box 120, S-671 23 ARVIKA, Sweden; 2001,* http://www.ncg.org/islam/Islam01-Allah.html.

7. Brother Andrew, *Islam: Truth or Myth?* Archaeological photo gallery of the Arabian Moon-God, http://www.bible.ca/islam/islam-photos-moon-worship-archealolgy.htm.

8. New Covenant Ministries, *The True Origin of 'Allah': The Archaeological Record Speaks,* http://www.nccg.org/islam/Islam01-Allah.html.

9. Ibid.

10. Ibid.

11. Ibid.

12. Morey, *Islamic Invasion,* 211–213.

13. Ibid., 215.

14. Ibid.

15. Warraq, *Why I Am Not a Muslim,* 34.

16. Brother Andrew, *Allah, the moon god of the Kaba,* www.bible.ca/islam/islam-moon-god-allah.htm.

17. John Van Ess, *Meet the Arab* (Museum Press, 1943), 29.

18. Egerton Sykes, *Everyman's Dictionary of Non-Classical Mythology, Allah,* (London: Dent, 1953), 7.

19. Warraq, *Why I Am Not a Muslim,* 42.

20. Martin Lings, *Muhammad: His Life Based on the Earliest Sources,* (Rochestor, VT: Inner Traditions International, LTD, 1983), 5.

21. Hafiz Ghulam Sarwar, *Muhammad, the Holy Prophet,* 18, 19.

22. Warraq, *Why I Am Not a Muslim,* 39.

23. Hafiz Ghulam Sarwar, *Muhammad, the Holy Prophet,* 18, 19.

24. Peter Occhiogrosso, *The Joy of Sects,* (New York, NY: Doubleday, Inc. 1997), 399.

25. Warraq, *Why I Am Not a Muslim,* 39.

26. George W. Braswell, Jr., *Islam Its Prophets, Peoples, Politics and Power,* (Nashville, TN: Broadman & Holman Publishers, 1996), 44.

27. Khairt al-Saeh, *Fabled Cities, Princes, and Jin from Arab Myths and Legends,* (from Brother Andrew: www.bible.ca/islam/islam-moon-god-hubal.htm 1985), 28–30.

28. Sam Chamoun, *Did the Meccans Worship Yahweh God? Revisiting the Issue of the Ishmaelites and the worship of the true God*, www.answering-islam.org.uk/Shamoun/ishmael-baal.htm .

29. Albert Hourani, *A History of Arab Peoples*, (New York, NY: Warner Books Edition, paperback, 1992), 16.

30. Samuel M Zwemer, *The Moslem Doctrine of God, An Essay on the Character and Attributes of Allah According to the Koran and Orthodox Tradition*, (www.bible.ca/islam/library/Zwemer/God/chap2.htm, 1905), 24–25.

31. Warraq, *Why I Am Not a Muslim*, 42.

32. W. Montgomery Watt, *Muhammad's Mecca* (Edinburgh: Edinburgh University Press, 1989), 26–45.

33. Karen Armstrong, *Muhammad: A Biography of the Prophet*, (San Francisco: Harper Collins Publishers, 1992) 69.

34. Carl Brockelmann, *History of the Islamic Peoples*, (New York, NY: Capricorn Books) 8–10.

35. Karen Armstrong, *Islam, A Short History*, (New York, NY: The Modern Library, 2002), 11

36. Kenneth Cragg, *The Call of The Minaret*, (New York, NY: Oxford University Press, 1956), 35–41

37. Armstrong, *Islam, A Short History*, 4

38. Warraq, *Why I Am Not a Muslim*, 42.

39. Ibid.

40. Morey, *The Islamic Invasion*, 218.

41. Philip K. Hitti, *History of the Arabs* (New York, NY: Palgrave MacMillan, 1937), 96–101.

42. Warraq, *Why I Am Not a Muslim*, 65.

43. Ibid.

44. B. Lewis, V.L. Menage, C. Pellat, J. Schacht, eds., *Encyclopedia of Islam*, Vol I. 303.

45. Jack Finegan, *The Archeology of World Religions* (Princeton, NJ:Princeton University Press, 1952), 482–485, 492.

46. Brother Andrew, *Islam: Truth or Myth? Modern usage of the moon god symbol in Islam and Arab nations*, http://www.bible.ca/islam/islam-allah-moon-god-symbols-modern.htm.

47. Caesar E. Farah, *Islam*, 6th ed. (Hauppaugo, NY: Barron's Educational Series, 2000), 28.

48. Warraq, *Why I Am Not a Muslim*, 36.

49. Ibid., 35.

50. Muir, The Apology of Al Kindy, 41, http://www.muhammadanism .com/Al-Kindi/al-kindi.pdf.

51. Farah, *Islam*, 28.

52. Jomier, *How to Understand Islam*, 70, 71.

53. M. J. Afshari, *Is Allah the Same God as the God of the Bible?* 6, 8–9, from Brother Andrew: http://www.bible.ca/islam/islam-allahs-daughters. htm.

54. Tanagho, *Glad News! God Loves You, My Muslim Friend*, 108.

## CHAPTER SIX
# Are Muslim Customs and Beliefs from God?

1. Lammens, *The Quest for the Historical Mohammad*, 282.

2. Sproul and Saleeb, *The Dark Side of Islam* (Wheaton, IL: Crossway Books, 84.

3. Irshad Manji, *The Trouble with Islam: A Muslim's Call for Reform in Her Faith* (New York, NY: St. Martin's Press, 2003), 151, 152, 155.

4. Ibid., 13, 155, 196.

5. Tommy Calvert Jr., "The American Anti-Slavery Group." Interview with Bill O'Reilly on *The O'Reilly Factor*, Fox News Channel, 24 June 2004.

6. Fox News, 1 August 2004.

7. Suzan Fraser, "EU Urges Turkey to Toughen Penalties for 'Honor' Killings," Assoc. Press (7 May 2004), http://www.islamreview.com/ news/2004_news2a.htm (accessed 1 August 2004).

8. Sahih Bukhari, Hadith, vol. 4, bk. 63, no. 260, http://www.use .edu/dept/MSA/reference/searchhadith.html (accessed 1 August 2004).

9. IranianVoice.org, from Al-Sharq Al-Awsat (London), 29 July 2003, http://www.a-listonline.com/iran/html/article1049.html (accessed 4 August 2003).

10. Ali Akbar Dareini, "Iran Frees Twice-Condemned Professor," Assoc. Press, 31 July 2004.

11. Muir, The Apology of Al Kindy, 28, 36. http://www.muhammadanism.com/Al-Kindi/al-kindi.pdf.

12. Norman L. Geisler, and Paul K. Hoffman, eds., *Why I Am a Christian: Why I Believe Jesus Christ Is the Ultimate Source of Meaning* by Ravi Zacharias (Grand Rapids: Baker, 2001), 269.

13. Ibid., 280.

14. Sproul and Saleeb, *The Dark Side of Islam*, 59, 63.

15. Tanagho, *Glad News! God Loves You, My Muslim Friend* (Waynesboro, GA: Authentic Media, 2003), 122.

16. Sproul and Saleeb, *Dark Side of Islam*, 64.

## CHAPTER SEVEN
## The Finale

1. Swindoll, *Swindoll's Ultimate Book of Illustrations and Quotes*, 313.

2. Lee Strobel, *The Case for Christ: A Journalist's Personal Investigation of the Evidence for Jesus* (Grand Rapids: Zondervan, 1998), 131.

3. Jomier, *How to Understand Islam*, 137.

4. Ibid.

5. Ibid.

6. Muir, Apology of Al Kindy, 28, 36.

7. Lammens, *The Quest for the Historical Mohammad*, 279.

8. Adrian Rogers, *Love Worth Finding*, television broadcast, Summer 2003, www.lwf.org .